THE ASTRAL PLANE

It's Scenery
Inhabitants
And
Phenomena

by
C. W. Leadbeater

Edited by Dr. Jane Ma'ati Smith

ISBN #1438262345 and EAN-13 # 9781438262345

CONTENTS

CHAPTER I
A GENERAL SURVEY

THOUGH for the most part entirely unconscious of it, man passes the whole of his life in the midst of a vast and populous unseen world. During sleep or in trance, when the insistent physical senses are for the time in abeyance, this other world is to some extent open to him, and he will sometimes bring back from those conditions more or less vague memories of what he has seen and heard there. When, at the change which men call death, he lays aside his physical body altogether, it is into this unseen world that he passes, and in it he lives through the long centuries that intervene between his incarnations into this existence that we know. By far the greater part of these long periods is spent in the heaven-world, to which the sixth of these manuals is devoted; but what we have now to consider is the lower part of this unseen world, the state into which man enters immediately after death – the Hades or underworld of the Greeks, the purgatory or intermediate state of Christianity which was called by mediæval alchemists the astral plane.

The object of this manual is to collect and arrange the information with regard to this interesting region which is scattered through Theosophical literature, and also to supplement it slightly in cases where new facts have come to our knowledge. It must be understood that any such additions are only the result of the investigations of a few explorers, and must not, therefore, be taken as in any way authoritative, but are given simply for what they are worth.

On the other hand every precaution in our power has been taken to ensure accuracy, no fact, old or new, being admitted to this manual unless it has been confirmed by the testimony of at least two independent trained investigators among ourselves, and has also been passed as correct by older students whose knowledge on these points is necessarily much greater than ours. It is hoped, therefore, that this

account of the astral plane, though it cannot be considered as quite complete, may yet be found reliable as far as it goes.
[Thus I wrote some forty years ago in the first edition of this book; now I may add that daily experience during the whole of that time has but confirmed the accuracy of last century's investigations. Much that was then still somewhat strange and novel has now become familiar through constant and intimate acquaintance, and a mass of additional evidence has been accumulated; here and there there may be a few words to add; there is practically nothing to alter.]

The first point which it is necessary to make clear in describing this astral plane is its absolute *reality*. In using that word I am not speaking from that metaphysical standpoint from which all but the One Unmanifested is unreal because impermanent; I am using the word in its plain, every-day sense, and I mean by it that the objects and inhabitants of the astral plane are real in exactly the same way as our own bodies, our furniture, our houses or monuments are real – as real as Charing Cross, to quote an expressive remark from one of the earliest Theosophical works. They will no more endure for ever than will objects on the physical plane, but they are nevertheless realities from our point of view while they last – realities which we cannot afford to ignore merely because the majority of mankind is as yet unconscious, or but vaguely conscious, of their existence. I know how difficult it is for the average mind to grasp the reality of that which we cannot see with our physical eyes. It is hard for us to realize how partial our sight is – to understand that we are all the time living in a vast world of which we see only a tiny part. Yet science tells us with no uncertain voice that this is so, for it describes to us whole worlds of minute life of whose existence we are entirely ignorant as far as our senses are concerned. Nor are the creatures of these worlds unimportant because minute, for upon a knowledge of the habits and condition of some of those microbes depends our ability to preserve health, and in many cases life itself.

In another direction also our senses are limited. We cannot see the very air that surrounds us; our senses give us no indication of its existence, except that when it is in motion we are aware of it by the sense of touch. Yet in it there is a force that can wreck our mightiest vessels and throw down our strongest buildings. Clearly all about us there are potent forces, which yet elude our poor and partial senses; so obviously we must beware of falling into the fatally common error of supposing that what *we* see is all there *is* to see.

We are, as it were, shut up in a tower, and our senses are tiny windows opening out in certain directions. In many other directions we are entirely shut in, but clairvoyance or astral sight opens for us one or two additional windows, and so enlarges our prospect, and spreads before us a new and wider world, which is yet part of the old world, though before we did not know it.

No one can get a clear conception of the teachings of the Wisdom-Religion until he has at any rate an intellectual grasp of the fact that in our solar system there exist perfectly definite planes, each with its own matter of different degrees of density. Some of these planes can be visited and observed by persons who have qualified themselves for the work, exactly as a foreign country might be visited and observed; and, by comparing the observations of those who are constantly working on these planes, evidence can be obtained of their existence and nature at least as satisfactory as that which most of us have for the existence of Greenland or Spitzbergen. Furthermore, just as any man who has the means and chooses to take the trouble can go and see Greenland or Spitzbergen for himself, so any man who chooses to take the trouble to qualify himself by living the necessary life, can in time come to see these higher planes on his own account.

The names usually given to these planes, taking them in order of materiality, rising from the denser to the finer, are the Physical, the Astral, the Mental or Devachanic, the Buddhic, and the Nirvanic. Higher than this last are two others, but they are so far above our present power of conception that for the moment they may be left out of consideration. It should be understood that the matter of each of these planes differs from that of the one below it in the same way as, though to a much greater degree than, vapour differs from solid matter; in fact, the states of matter which we call solid, liquid, and gaseous are merely the three lowest sub-divisions of the matter belonging to this one physical plane.

The astral region which I am to attempt to describe is the second of these great Planes of Nature – the next above (or within) that physical world with which we are all familiar. It has often been called the realm of illusion – not that it is itself any more illusory than the physical world, but, because of the extreme unreliability of the impressions brought back from it by the untrained seer.

Why should this be so? We account for it mainly by two remarkable characteristics of the astral world – first, that many of its inhabitants have a marvellous power of changing their forms with Protean rapidity, and also of casting practically unlimited glamour over those with whom they choose to sport; and secondly, that sight on that plane is a faculty very different from and much more extended than physical vision. An object is seen, as it were, from all sides at once, the inside of a solid being as plainly open to the view as the outside; it is therefore obvious that an inexperienced visitor to this new world may well find considerable difficulty in understanding what he really does see, and still more in translating his vision into the very inadequate language of ordinary speech.

A good example of the sort of mistake that is likely to occur is the frequent reversal of any number which the seer has to read from the astral light, so that he would be liable to render, say, 139 as 931, and so on. In the case of a student of occultism trained by a capable Master such a mistake would be impossible except through great hurry or carelessness, since such a pupil has to go through a long and varied course of instruction in this art of seeing correctly. The Master, or perhaps some more advanced pupil, brings before him again and again all possible forms of illusion, and asks him "What do you see?" Any errors in his answers are then corrected and their reasons explained, until by degrees the neophyte acquires a certainty and confidence in dealing with the phenomena of the astral plane which far exceeds anything possible in physical life.

He has to learn not only to see correctly but to translate accurately, from one plane to the other the memory of what he has seen. To assist him in this he has eventually to learn to carry his consciousness without break from the physical plane to the astral or mental and back again, for until that can be done there is always a possibility that his recollections may be partially lost or distorted during the blank interval which separates his periods of consciousness on the various planes. When the power of bringing over the consciousness is perfectly acquired the pupil will have the advantage of the use of all the astral faculties, not only while out of his body during sleep or trance, but also while fully awake in ordinary physical life.

It has been the custom of some Theosophists to speak with scorn of the astral plane, and treat it as entirely unworthy of attention; but that seems to me a mistaken view. Assuredly, that at which we have to aim is the life of the spirit, and it would be most disastrous for any student to neglect that higher development and rest satisfied with the attainment of astral consciousness. There have been some whose karma was such as to enable them to develop the higher mental faculties first of all – to overleap the astral plane for the time, as it were; but this is not the ordinary method adopted by the Masters of Wisdom with their pupils.

Where it is possible it no doubt saves trouble, for the higher usually includes the lower; but for most of us such progress by leaps and bounds has been forbidden by our own faults or follies in the past; all that we can hope for is to win our way slowly step by step, and since this astral plane lies next to our world of denser matter, it is usually in connection with it that our earliest super-physical experiences take place. It is therefore of deep interest to those of us who are but beginners in these studies, and a clear comprehension of its mysteries may often be of the greatest importance to us, by enabling us not only to understand many of the phenomena of the *séance*-room, of haunted houses, etc., which would otherwise be inexplicable, but also to guard ourselves and others from possible dangers.

The first conscious introduction to this remarkable region comes to people in various ways. Some only once in their whole lives under some unusual influence become sensitive enough to recognize the presence of one of its inhabitants, and perhaps, because the experience does not repeat itself, they may come in time to believe that on that occasion they must have been the victims of hallucination. Others find themselves with increasing frequency seeing and hearing something to which those around them are blind and deaf; others again – and perhaps this is the commonest experience of all – begin to recollect with greater and greater clearness that which they have seen or heard on that other plane during sleep.

It must be understood that the power of objective perception upon all the planes undoubtedly lies latent in every man, but for most of us it will be a matter of long and slow evolution before our consciousness can fully function in those higher vehicles. With regard to the astral body the matter is, however, somewhat different, for in the case of all the cultured people belonging to the more advanced races of the world, the consciousness is already perfectly capable not only of responding to all vibrations communicated to it through astral matter, but also of using its astral body definitely as a vehicle and instrument.

Most of us, then, are awake on the astral plane during the sleep of the physical body, and yet we are generally very little awake *to* the plane, and are consequently conscious of our surroundings there only vaguely, if at all. We are still wrapped up in our waking thoughts and our physical-plane affairs, and we pay scarcely any attention to the world of intensely active life that surrounds us. Our first step, then, is to shake off this habit of thought, and learn to see that new and beautiful world, so that we may be able intelligently to work in it. Even when that is achieved, it does not necessarily follow that we shall be able to bring over into our waking consciousness any recollection of those astral experiences. But that question of physical-plane remembrance is an entirely different matter, and does not in any way affect our power to do excellent astral work.

Among those who make a study of these subjects, some try to develop the astral sight by crystal-gazing or other methods, while those who have the inestimable advantage of the direct guidance of a qualified teacher will probably be aroused to full consciousness upon that plane for the first time under his special protection, which will be continued until, by the application of various tests, he has satisfied himself that each pupil is proof against any danger or terror that he is likely to encounter. But however it may occur, the first actual realization that we are all the while in the midst of a great world full of active life, of which most of us are nevertheless entirely unconscious, cannot but be a memorable epoch in a man's existence.

So abundant and so manifold is this life of the astral plane that at first it is absolutely bewildering to the neophyte; and even for the more practised investigator it is no easy task to attempt to classify and to catalogue it. If the explorer of some unknown tropical forest were asked not only to give a full account of the country through which he has passed, with accurate details of its vegetable and mineral productions, but also to state the genus and species of every one of the myriad insects, birds, beasts, and reptiles which he had seen, he might well shrink appalled at the magnitude of the undertaking. Yet even this affords no parallel to the embarrassments of the psychic investigator, for in his case matters are further complicated, first by the difficulty of correctly translating from that plane to this the recollection of what he has seen, and secondly by the utter inadequacy of ordinary language to express much of what he has to report.

However, just as the explorer on the physical plane would probably commence his account of a country by some sort of general description of its scenery and characteristics, so it will be well to begin this slight sketch of the astral plane by endeavouring to give some idea of the scenery which forms the background of its marvelous and ever-changing activities. Yet here at the outset an almost insuperable difficulty confronts us in the extreme complexity of the matter. All who see fully on that plane agree that to attempt to call up a vivid picture of this astral scenery before those whose eyes are as yet unopened is like speaking to a blind man of the exquisite variety of tints in a sunset sky – however detailed and elaborate the description may be, there is no certainty that the idea presented before the hearer's mind will be an adequate representation of the truth.

CHAPTER II
SCENERY

FIRST of all, then, it must be understood that the astral plane has seven subdivisions, each of which has its corresponding degree of materiality and its corresponding condition of matter. Although the poverty of physical language forces us to speak of these sub-planes as higher and lower, we must not fall into the mistake of thinking of them (or indeed of the greater planes of which they are only subdivisions) as separate localities in space – as lying above one another like the shelves of a book-case or outside one another like the coats of an onion. It must be understood that the matter of each plane or sub-plane interpenetrates that of the plane or sub-plane below it, so that here at the surface of the earth all exist together in the same space, although it is true that the higher varieties of matter extend further away from the physical earth than the lower.

So when we speak of a man as rising from one plane or sub-plane to another, we do not think of him as necessarily moving in space at all, but rather as transferring his consciousness from one level to another – gradually becoming unresponsive to the vibrations of one order of matter, and beginning instead to answer to those of a higher and more refined order; so that one world with its scenery and inhabitants would seem to fade slowly away from his view, while another world of a more elevated character dawns upon him in its stead.

Yet there is a point of view from which there is a certain justification for the use of the terms "higher" and "lower", and for the comparison of the planes and sub-planes to concentric shells. Matter of all the sub-planes is to be found here on the surface of the earth, but the astral plane is much larger than the physical, and extends some thousands of miles above its surface. The law of gravitation operates on astral matter, and if it were possible for it to be left entirely undisturbed it *would* probably settle into concentric shells. But the earth is in perpetual motion, both of rotation and revolution, and all kinds of influences and forces are continually rushing about, so this ideal condition of rest is never attained, and there is much intermingling. Nevertheless it remains true that the higher we rise the less of the denser matter do we find.

We have a fair analogy on the physical plane. Earth, water and air – the solid, the liquid and the gaseous – all exist here on the surface, but broadly speaking it is true to say the solid matter lies lowest, the liquid next to it, and the gaseous matter higher still. Water and air interpenetrate the earth to a small extent; water also rises in the air in the shape of clouds, but only to a limited height; solid matter may be thrown up into the air by violent convulsions, as in the great eruption of Krakatoa in 1883, when the volcanic dust reached the height of seventeen miles, and took three years to settle down again; but it *does* settle down eventually, just as the water drawn up into the air by evaporation returns to us as rain. The higher we rise the more rarefied does the air become; and the same is true with regard to astral matter.

The dimensions of our astral world are considerable, and we are able to determine them with some approach to accuracy from the fact that our astral world touches that of the moon at perigee, but does not reach it at apogee; but naturally the contact is confined to the highest type of astral matter.

Returning to the consideration of these sub-planes, and numbering them from the highest and least material downwards, we find that they naturally fall into three classes, divisions 1, 2 and 3 forming one such class, and 4, 5 and 6 another, while the seventh and lowest of all stands alone. The difference between the matter of one of these classes and the next would be commensurable with that between a solid and a liquid, while the difference between the matter of the subdivisions of a class would rather resemble that between two kinds of solid, such as, say, steel and sand. Putting aside for the moment the seventh, we may say that divisions 4, 5 and 6 of the astral plane have for their background the physical world in which we live, and all its familiar accessories. Life on the sixth division is not unlike our ordinary life on this earth, minus the physical body and its necessities; while as it ascends through the fifth and fourth divisions it becomes less and less material, and is more and more withdrawn from our lower world and its interests.

The scenery of these lower divisions, then, is that of the earth as we know it; but in reality it is also much more: for when we look at it from this different standpoint, with the assistance of the astral senses, even purely physical objects present quite a different appearance. As has already been mentioned, one whose eyes are fully opened sees them, not as usual from one point of view, but from all sides at once – an idea in itself sufficiently confusing.

When we add to this that every particle in the interior of a solid body is as fully and clearly visible as those on the outside, it will be comprehended that under such conditions even the most familiar objects may at first be totally unrecognizable.

Yet a moment's consideration will show that such vision approximates much more closely to true perception than does physical sight. Looked at on the astral plane, for example, the sides of a glass cube would all appear equal, as they really are, while on the physical plane we see the further side in perspective – that is, it appears smaller than the nearer side, which is a mere illusion. It is this characteristic of astral vision which has led some writers to describe it as sight in the fourth dimension – a suggestive and expressive phrase.

In addition to these possible sources of error, matters are further complicated by the fact that this higher sight cognizes forms of matter which, while still purely physical,

14

are nevertheless invisible under ordinary conditions. Such, for example, are the particles composing the atmosphere, all the various emanations which are always being given out by everything that has life, and also four grades of a still finer order of physical matter which, for want of more distinctive names, are usually described as 'etheric'. The latter form a kind of system by themselves, freely interpenetrating all other physical matter; and the investigation of their vibrations and the manner in which various higher forces affect them would in itself constitute a vast field of deeply interesting study for any man of science who possessed the requisite sight for its examination.

Even when our imagination has fully grasped all that is comprehended in what has already been said, we do not yet understand half the complexity of the problem for besides all these new forms of physical matter we have to deal with the still more numerous and perplexing subdivisions of astral matter. We must note first that every material object, every particle even, has its astral counterpart; and this counterpart is itself not a simple body, but is usually extremely complex, being composed of various kinds of astral matter. In addition to this each living creature is surrounded with an atmosphere of its own, usually called its aura, and in the case of human beings this aura forms of itself a very fascinating branch of study. It is seen as an oval mass of luminous mist of highly complex structure, and from its shape has sometimes been called the auric egg.

Theosophical readers will hear with pleasure that even at the early stage of his development at which the pupil begins to acquire this fuller sight, he is able to assure himself by direct observation of the accuracy of the teaching given through our great founder, Madame Blavatsky, on the subject of some at least of the "seven principles of man." In regarding his fellow-man he no longer sees only his outer appearance; almost exactly co-extensive with that physical body he clearly distinguishes the etheric double; while the vitality (called in Sanskrit *prana*) is also obvious as it is absorbed and specialized, as it circulates in rosy light throughout the body, as it eventually radiates from the healthy person in its altered form.

Most brilliant and most easily seen of all, perhaps, though belonging to a more refined order of matter – the astral – is that part of the aura which expresses by its vivid and ever-changing flashes of colour the different desires which sweep across the man's mind from moment to moment. This is the true astral body. Behind that, and consisting of a finer grade of matter again – that of the form-levels of the mental plane – lies the mental body or aura of the lower mind, whose colours, changing only by slow degrees as the man lives his life, show the trend of his thoughts and the disposition and character of his personality. Still higher and infinitely more beautiful, where at all clearly developed, is the living light of the causal body, the vehicle of the higher self, which shows the stage of development of the real ego its passage from birth to birth. But to see these the pupil must, of course, have developed the vision of the levels to which they belong.

It will save the student much trouble if he learns at once to regard these auras not as mere emanations, but as the actual manifestation of the ego on their respective planes – if he understands that it is the ego, which is the real man, not the various bodies which on the lower planes represent him. So long as the reincarnating ego remains upon the plane which is his true home in the formless levels, the vehicle which he inhabits is the causal body, but when he descends into the form-level he must, in order to be able to function upon them, clothe himself in their matter; and the matter that he thus attracts to himself furnishes his mind-body.

Similarly, descending into the astral plane he forms his astral or desire-body out of its matter, though still retaining all the other bodies, and on his still further descent to this lowest plane of all the physical body is formed according to the etheric mould supplied by the Lords of Karma. Fuller accounts of these auras will be found in my book *Man, Visible and Invisible*, but enough has been said here to show that as they all occupy the same space, the finer interpenetrating the grosser, it needs careful study and much practice to enable the neophyte to distinguish clearly at a glance the one from the other. Nevertheless the human aura, or more usually some one part of it only, is not infrequently one of the first purely astral objects seen by the untrained, though in such a case its indications are naturally likely to be misunderstood.

Though the astral aura from the brilliancy of its flashes of colour may often be more conspicuous, the nerve-ether and the etheric double are really of a much denser order of matter, being within the limits of the physical plane, though invisible to ordinary sight. If we examine with psychic faculty the body of a newly-born child, we shall find it permeated not only by astral matter of every degree of density, but also by the several grades of etheric matter. If we take the trouble to trace these inner bodies backwards to their origin, we find that it is of the latter that the etheric double – the mould upon which the physical body is built up – is formed by the agents of the Lords of Karma; while the astral matter has been gathered together by the descending ego, not consciously, but automatically, as he passes through the astral plane.

Into the composition of the etheric double must enter something of all the different grades of etheric matter; but the proportions may vary greatly, and are determined by several factors, such as the race, sub-race, and type of a man, as well as by his individual karma. When it is remembered that these four subdivisions of matter are made up of numerous combinations, which, in their turn, form aggregations that enter into the composition of the "atom" of the so-called "element" of the chemist, it will be seen that this second principle of man is highly complex, and the number of its possible variations practically infinite. So that, however complicated and unusual a man's karma may be, those in whose province such work falls are able to give a mould in accordance with which a body exactly suiting it can be formed. But for information upon this vast subject of karma the previous manual should be consulted.

One other point deserves mention in connection with the appearance of physical matter when looked at from the astral plane, and that is that the higher vision, when fully developed, possesses the power of magnifying at will the minutest physical particle to any desired size, as though by a microscope, though its magnifying power is enormously greater than that of any microscope ever made or ever likely to be made. The hypothetical molecules and atoms postulated by science are visible realities to the occult student, though the latter recognizes them as much more complex in their nature than the scientific man has yet discovered them to be. Here again is a vast field of study of absorbing interest to which a whole volume might readily be devoted; and a scientific investigator who should acquire this astral sight in perfection, would not only find his experiments with ordinary and known phenomena immensely facilitated, but would also see stretching before him entirely new vistas of knowledge needing more than a lifetime for their thorough examination.

For example, one curious and beautiful novelty brought to his notice by the development of this vision would be the existence of other and entirely different colours beyond the limits of the ordinarily visible spectrum, the ultra-red and ultra-violet rays which science has discovered by other means being plainly perceptible to astral sight. We must not, however, allow ourselves to follow these fascinating bye-paths, but must resume our endeavour to give a general idea of the appearance of the astral plane.

It will by this time be obvious that though, as above stated, the ordinary objects of the physical world form the background to life on certain levels of the astral plane, yet so much more is seen of their real appearance and characteristics that the general effect differs widely from that with which we are familiar. For the sake of illustration take a rock as an example of the simpler class of objects. When regarded with trained sight it is no mere inert mass of stone. First of all, the whole of the physical matter of the rock is seen, instead of a small part of it; secondly, the vibrations of its physical particles are perceptible; thirdly, it is seen to possess an astral counterpart composed of various grades of astral matter, whose particles are also in constant motion; fourthly, the Universal Divine Life is clearly to be seen working in it as it works in the whole creation, though naturally its manifestations differ greatly at successive stages of its descent into matter, and for the sake of convenience

18

each stage has its own name. We recognize it first in the three elemental kingdoms; when it enters the mineral kingdom we call it the mineral monad; in the vegetable kingdom it is described as the vegetable monad, and so on. So far as we know, there is no such thing as "dead" matter.

In addition to all this an aura will be seen surrounding it, though this is much less extended and varied than in the case of the higher kingdoms; and its appropriate elemental inhabitants may be seen – though these should more properly be described as gnomes, a variety of nature-spirit. This is not the place to treat fully the subject of the Indwelling Life; further explanations will be found in *Man, Visible and Invisible* and other Theosophical works. Also see a later chapter of this book. In the case of the vegetable, animal, and human kingdoms, the complications are naturally much more numerous.

It may be objected by some readers that no such complexities as these are described by most of the psychics who occasionally catch glimpses of the astral world, nor are they reported at *séances* by the entities that manifest there; but we can readily account for this. Few untrained persons on that plane, whether living or dead, see things as they really are until after long experience; even those who do see fully are often too dazed and confused to understand or remember; and among the small minority who both see and remember there are hardly any who can translate the recollection into language on our lower plane. Many untrained psychics never examine their visions scientifically at all; they just obtain an impression which may be quite correct, but may also be half false, or even wholly misleading.

All the more probable does the latter hypothesis become when we take into consideration the frequent tricks played by sportive denizens of the other world, against which the untrained person is usually absolutely defenceless. It must also be remembered that the regular inhabitant of the astral plane is under ordinary circumstances conscious only of the objects of that plane, physical matter being to him as entirely invisible as is astral matter to the majority of mankind.

Since, as before remarked, every physical object has its astral counterpart, which *is* visible to him, it may be thought that the distinction is trivial, yet it is an essential part of the symmetrical conception of the subject.

If, however, an astral entity constantly works through a medium, these finer astral senses may gradually be so coarsened as to become insensible to the higher grades of matter on their own plane, and to include in their purview the physical world as we see it instead; but only the trained visitor from this life; who is fully conscious on both planes, can depend upon seeing both clearly and simultaneously. Be it understood, then, that the complexity exists, and that only when it is fully perceived and scientifically unraveled is there perfect security against deception or mistake.

For the seventh or lowest subdivision of the astral plane also, this physical world of ours may be said to be the background, though what is seen is only a distorted and partial view of it, since all that is light and good and beautiful seems invisible. It was thus described four thousand years ago in the Egyptian papyrus of the Scribe Ani: "What manner of place is this unto which I have come? It hath no water, it hath no air; it is deep, unfathomable; it is black as the blackest night, and men wander helplessly about therein; in it a man may not live in quietness of heart." For the unfortunate human being on that level it is indeed true that "all the earth is full of darkness and cruel habitations", but it is darkness which radiates from within himself and causes his existence to be passed in a perpetual night of evil and horror – a real hell, though, like all other hells, entirely of man's own creation.

I do not mean by this that the sub-plane is wholly imaginary – that it has no objective existence. It lies partly on the surface of the earth, and partly (perhaps mostly) *beneath* that surface, interpenetrating the solid crust. But I *do* mean that no man who lives an ordinarily pure and decent life need ever touch this eminently undesirable region, or even become conscious of its existence. If he *does* contact it, is entirely due to his own coarse and evil action, speech and thought.

20

Most students find the investigation of this section an extremely unpleasant task, for there appears to be a sense of density and gross materiality about it which is indescribably loathsome to the liberated astral body, causing it the feeling of pushing its way through some black, viscous fluid, while the inhabitants and influences encountered there are also usually exceedingly objectionable.

The first, second and third subdivisions, though occupying the same space, yet give the impression of being much further removed from this physical world, and correspondingly less material. Entities inhabiting these levels lose sight of the earth and its belongings; they are usually deeply self-absorbed, and to a large extent create their own surroundings, though these are sufficiently objective to be perceptible to other entities and also to clairvoyant vision. This region is the "summer-land" of which we hear so much at spiritualistic *séances,* and those who descend from and describe it no doubt speak the truth as far as their knowledge extends.

It is on these planes that "spirits" call into temporary existence their houses, schools, and cities, for these object are often real enough for the time, though to a clearer sight they may sometimes be pitiably unlike what their delighted creators suppose them to be. Nevertheless, many of the imaginations which take form there are of real though temporary beauty, and a visitor who knew of nothing higher might wander contentedly enough there among forests and mountains, lovely lakes and pleasant flower gardens, which are at any rate much superior to anything in the physical world; or he might even construct such surroundings to suit his own fancies. The details of the differences between these three higher sub-planes will perhaps be more readily explicable when we come to deal with their human inhabitants.

An account of the scenery of the astral plane would be incomplete without some mention of what have often, though mistakenly, been called the Records of the Astral Light. These records (which are in truth a sort of materialization of the Divine memory – a living photographic representation of all that has ever happened) are really and permanently impressed upon a very much higher level, and are only reflected in a more or less spasmodic manner on the astral plane, so that one whose power of vision does not rise above this will be likely to obtain only occasional and disconnected pictures of the past instead of a coherent narrative. But nevertheless these reflected pictures of all kinds of past events are constantly being reproduced in the astral world, and form an important part of the surroundings of the investigator there. I have not space to do more than just mention them here, but a fuller account of them will be found in Chapter vii of my little book on *Clairvoyance.*

CHAPTER III
INHABITANTS

HAVING sketched in, however slightly, the background of our picture, we must now attempt to fill in the figures – to describe the inhabitants of the astral plane. The immense variety of these beings makes it exceedingly difficult to arrange and tabulate them. Perhaps the most convenient method will be to divide them into three great classes, the human, the non-human, and the artificial.

I. HUMAN

The human denizens of the astral plane fall naturally into two groups, the living and the dead, or, to speak more accurately, those who have still a physical body, and those who have not.

1. Living
The men who manifest themselves on the astral plane during physical life may be subdivided into four classes:

1. *The Adept and his Pupils.* Those belonging to this class usually employ as a vehicle not the astral body at all, but the mind-body, which is composed of the matter of the four lower or rupa levels of the plane next above. The advantage of this vehicle is that it permits of instant passage from the mental plane to the astral and back, and allows of the use at all times of the greater power and keener sense of its own plane. The mind-body is not naturally visible to astral sight at all, and consequently the pupil who works in it learns to gather round himself a temporary veil of astral matter when in the course of his work he wishes to become perceptible to the inhabitants of the lower plane in order to help them more efficiently. This temporary body (called the *mayavirupa*) is usually formed for the pupil by his Master on the first occasion, and he is then instructed and assisted until he can form it for himself easily and expeditiously. Such a vehicle, though an exact reproduction of the man in appearance, contains none of the matter of his own astral body, but corresponds to it in the same way as a materialization corresponds to a physical body.

At an earlier stage of his development the pupil may be found functioning in the astral body like any one else; but whichever vehicle he is employing, the man who is introduced to the astral plane under the guidance of a competent teacher has always the fullest possible consciousness there, and is able to function perfectly easily upon all its subdivisions. He is in fact himself, exactly as his friends know him on earth, minus only the physical body and the etheric double in the one case and the astral body in addition to the other, and plus the additional powers and faculties of this higher condition, which enable him to carry on far more easily and far more efficiently on that plane during sleep the Theosophical work which occupies so much of his thought in his waking hours. Whether he will remember fully and accurately on the physical plane what he has done or learnt on the other depends largely upon whether he is able to carry his consciousness without intermission from the one state to the other.

The investigator will occasionally meet in the astral world students of occultism from all parts of the world (belonging to lodges quite unconnected with the Masters of whom Theosophists know most) who are in many cases most earnest and self-sacrificing seekers after truth. It is noteworthy, however, that all such lodges are at least aware of the existence of the great Himalayan Brotherhood, and acknowledge it as containing among its members the highest Adepts now known on earth.

2. *The Psychically-developed Person who is not under the guidance of a Master.* Such a person may or may not be spiritually developed, for the two forms of advancement do not necessarily go together. When a man is born with psychic powers it is simply the result of efforts made during a previous incarnation – efforts which may have been of the noblest and most unselfish character, or on the other hand may have been ignorant and ill-directed or even entirely unworthy.

Such a man is usually perfectly conscious when out of the body, but for want of proper training is liable to be greatly deceived as to what he sees. He is often able to range through the different subdivisions of the astral plane almost as fully as persons belonging to the last class; but sometimes he is especially attracted to some one division and rarely travels beyond its influences. His recollection of what he has seen may vary according to the degree of his development through all the stages from perfect clearness to utter distortion or blank oblivion. He always appears in his astral body, since he does not know how to function in the mental vehicle.

3. *The Ordinary Person* – that is, the person without any psychic development – who floats about in his astral body during sleep in a more or less unconscious condition. In deep slumber the higher principles in their astral vehicle almost invariably withdraw from the body, and hover in its immediate neighbourhood, though in quite undeveloped persons they are practically almost as much asleep as the body is.

In some cases, however, this astral vehicle is less lethargic, and floats dreamily about on the various astral currents, occasionally recognizing other people in a similar condition, and meeting with experiences of all sorts, pleasant and unpleasant, the memory of which, hopelessly confused and often travestied into a grotesque caricature of what really happened, will cause the man to think next morning what a remarkable dream he has had.

All cultured people, have at the present time their astral senses very fairly developed, so that, if they were sufficiently aroused to examine the realities which surround them during sleep, they would be able to observe them and learn much from them. But, in the vast majority of cases, they are not so aroused, and they spend most of their nights in a kind of brown study, pondering deeply over whatever thought may have been uppermost in their minds when they fell asleep. They have the astral faculties, but they scarcely use them; they are certainly awake on the astral plane, and yet they are not in the least awake *to* the plane, and are consequently conscious of their surroundings only very vaguely, if at all.

When such a man becomes a pupil of one of the Masters of Wisdom, he is usually at once shaken out of this somnolent condition, fully awakened to the realities around him on that plane, and set to learn from them and to work among them, so that his hours of sleep are no longer a blank, but are filled with active and useful occupation, without in the least interfering with the healthy, repose of the tired physical body.

These extruded astral bodies are almost shapeless and indefinite in outline in the case of the more backward races and individuals, but as the man develops in intellect and spirituality his floating astral becomes better defined, and more closely resembles his physical encasement. It is often asked how – since the undeveloped astral is so vague in outline, and since the great majority of mankind come under the head of the undeveloped – how it is ever possible to recognise the ordinary man at all when he is in his astral body. In trying to answer that question we must endeavour to realize that, to the clairvoyant eye, the physical body of man appears surrounded by what we call the aura – a luminous coloured mist, roughly ovoid in shape, and extending to a distance of some eighteen inches from the body in all directions. All students are aware that this aura is exceedingly complex, and contains matter of all the different planes on which man is at present provided with vehicles;

but for the moment let us think of it as it would appear to one who possessed no higher power of vision than the astral. For such a spectator the aura would contain only astral matter, and would therefore be a simpler object of study. He would see, however, that this astral matter not only surrounded the physical body, but interpenetrated it, and that within the periphery of that body it was much more densely aggregated than in that part of the aura which lay outside it. This seems to be due to the attraction of the large amount of dense astral matter which is gathered together there as the counterpart of the cells of the physical body; but however that may he, the fact is undoubted that the matter of the astral body which lies within the limits of the physical is many times denser than that outside it.

When during sleep the astral body is withdrawn from the physical this arrangement still persists, and any one looking at such an astral body with clairvoyant vision would still see, just as before, a form resembling the physical body surrounded by an aura. That form would is now composed only of astral matter, but still the difference in density between it and its surrounding mist would be quite sufficient to make it clearly distinguishable, even though it is itself only a form of denser mist.

Now as to the difference in appearance between the evolved and the unevolved man. Even in the case of the latter the features and shape of the inner forms are recognizable always, though blurred and indistinct, but the surrounding egg scarcely deserve the name, for it is in fact a mere shapeless wreath of mist, having neither regularity nor permanence of outline.

In the more developed man the change would be very marked, both in the aura and the form within it. This latter would be far more distinct and definite – a closer reproduction of the man's physical appearance; while instead of the floating mist-wreath we see a sharply defined ovoid shape, preserving this form unaffected amidst all the varied currents which are always swirling around it on the astral plane.

Since the psychical faculties of mankind are in course of evolution, and individuals are at all stages of their development, this class naturally melts by imperceptible gradations into the former.

4. *The Black Magician or his pupil.* This class corresponds somewhat to the first, except that the development has been for evil instead of good, and the powers acquired are used for purely selfish purposes instead of for the benefit of humanity. Among its lower ranks come members who practise the ghastly rites of the Obeah or Voodoo schools, and while higher in intellect, and therefore the more blameworthy, stand the Tibetan black magicians, who are often, though incorrectly, called by Europeans Dugpas – a title properly belonging, as is quite correctly explained by Surgeon-Major Waddell in his book on *The Buddhism of Tibet,* only to the Bhotanese subdivision of the great Kargyu sect, which is part of what may be called the semi-reformed school of Tibetan Buddhism.

The Dugpas no doubt deal in Tantrik magic to a considerable extent, but the real red-hatted entirely unreformed sect is that of the Nin-ma-pa, though far beyond them still lower depth be the Bonpa – the votaries of the aboriginal religion, who have never accepted any form of Buddhism at all. It must not, however, be supposed that all Tibetan sects except the Gelugpa are necessarily and altogether evil; a truer view would be that as the rules of other sects permit considerably greater laxity of life and practice, the proportion of self-seekers among them is likely to be much larger than among the stricter reformers.

2. Dead

First of all, this very word "dead" is an absurd misnomer, as most of the entities classified under this heading are as fully alive as we are ourselves – often distinctly more so; so the term must be understood simply as meaning those who are for the time unattached to a physical body. They may be subdivided into ten principal classes, as follows:

1. *The Nirmanakaya.* (one who, having earned the right to the perpetual enjoyment of Nirvana, renounces it in order to devote himself to work for the good of mankind). This class is just mentioned in order to make the catalogue complete, but it is rarely indeed that so exalted a being manifests himself upon so low a plane as this. When for any reason connected with his sublime work he found it desirable to do so, he would probably create a temporary astral body for the purpose from the atomic matter of the plane, just as the Adept in the mind-body would do, simply because his more refined vesture would be invisible to astral sight. In order to be able to function without a moment's hesitation on any plane, he retains always within himself some atoms belonging to each, round which as a nucleus he can instantly aggregate other matter, and so provide himself with whatever vehicle he desires.

2. *The Pupil awaiting reincarnation.* It has frequently been stated in Theosophical literature that when the pupil reaches a certain stage he is able with the assistance of his Master to escape from the action of what is in ordinary cases the law of Nature which carries a human being into the heaven-world at the end of his astral life. In that heaven-world he would, in the ordinary course of events, receive the due result of the full working out of all the spiritual forces, which his highest aspirations have set in motion while on earth.

As the pupil must by the hypothesis be a man of pure life and high thought, it is probable that in his case these spiritual forces will be of abnormal strength, and therefore if he enters upon this heaven-life, it is likely to be extremely long; but if instead of taking it he chooses the Path of Renunciation (thus even at his low level and in his humble way beginning to follow in the footsteps of the Great Master of Renunciation, the Lord GAUTAMA Buddha Himself), he is able to expend that reserve of force in quite another direction – to use it for the benefit of mankind, and so, infinitesimal though his offering may be, to take his tiny part in the great work of the Nirmanakayas. By taking this course he no doubt sacrifices centuries of intense bliss, but on the other hand he gains the enormous advantage of being able to continue his life of work and progress without a break.

28

When a pupil who has decided to do this dies, he simply steps out of his body, as he has often done before, and waits upon the astral plane until a suitable reincarnation can be arranged for him by his Master. This being a marked departure from the usual course of procedure, the permission of a very high authority has to be obtained before the attempt can be made; yet, even when this is granted, so strong is the force of natural law, that it is said the pupil must be careful to confine himself strictly to the astral level while the matter is being arranged, lest if he once, even for a moment, touched the mental plane, he might be swept as by an irresistible current into the line of normal evolution again. In some cases, though these are rare, he is enabled to avoid the trouble of a new birth by being placed directly in an adult body whose previous tenant has no further use for it, but naturally it is not often that a suitable body is available. Far more frequently he has to wait on the astral plane, as mentioned before, until the opportunity of a fitting birth presents itself. Meanwhile, however, he is losing no time, for he is as fully himself as ever he was, and is able to go on with the work given him by his Master even more quickly and efficiently than when in the physical body, since he is no longer hampered by the possibility of fatigue. His consciousness is quite complete, and he roams at will through all the divisions of the plane with equal facility.

The pupil awaiting reincarnation is by no means one of the common objects of the astral plane, but still he may be met with occasionally, and therefore he forms one of our classes. No doubt as the evolution of humanity proceeds, and an ever-increasing proportion enters upon the Path of Holiness, this class will become more numerous.

3. *The Ordinary Person after death.* Needless to say this class is millions of times larger than those of which we have spoken, and the character and condition of its members vary within extremely wide limits. Within similarly wide limits may vary also the length of their lives upon the astral plane, for while there are those who pass only a few days or hours there, others remain upon this level for many years and even centuries.

A man who has led a good and pure life, whose strongest feelings and aspirations have been unselfish and spiritual, will have no attraction to this plane, and will, if entirely left alone, find little to keep him upon it, or to awaken him into activity even during the comparatively short period of his stay. For it must be understood that after death the true man is withdrawing into himself, and just as at the first step of that process he casts off the physical body, and almost directly afterwards the etheric double, so it is intended that he should as soon as possible cast off also the astral or desire body, and pass into the heaven-world, where alone his spiritual aspirations can bear their perfect fruit.

The noble and pure-minded man will be able to do this, for he has subdued all earthly passions during life; the force of his will has been directed into higher channels, and there is therefore but little energy of lower desire to be worked out on the astral plane. His stay there will consequently be short, and most probably he will have little more than a dreamy half-consciousness of existence until he sinks into the sleep during which his higher principles finally free themselves from the astral envelope and enter upon the blissful life of the heaven-world.

For the person who has not as yet entered upon the path of occult development, what has been described is the ideal state of affairs, but naturally it not attained by all, or even by the majority. The average man has by no means freed himself from all lower desires before death, and it takes a long period of more or less fully conscious life on the various subdivisions of the astral plane to allow the forces, which he has generated to work themselves out, and thus release the ego.

Every one after death has to pass through all the subdivisions of the astral plane on his way to the heaven-world, though it must not be inferred that he will be conscious upon all of them. Precisely as it is necessary that the physical body should contain within its constitution physical matter in all its conditions, solid, liquid, gaseous, and etheric, so it is indispensable that the astral vehicle should contain particles belonging to all the corresponding subdivisions of astral matter, though the proportions may vary greatly in different cases.

It must be remembered that along with the matter of his astral body a man picks up the corresponding elemental essence, and that during his life this essence is segregated from the ocean of similar matter around, and practically becomes for that time what may be described as a kind of artificial elemental. This has temporarily a definite separate existence of its own, and follows the course of its own evolution downwards into matter without any reference to (or indeed any knowledge of) the convenience or interest of the ego to whom it happens to be attached – thus causing that perpetual struggle between the will of the flesh and the will of the spirit to which religious writers so often refer.

Yet though it is "a law of the members warring against the law of the mind", though if the man obeys it instead of controlling it his evolution will be seriously hindered, it must not be thought of as in any way evil in itself, for it is still a Law – still an outpouring of the Divine Power going on its orderly course, though that course in this instance happens to be downwards into matter instead of upwards and away from it, as ours is.

When the man passes away at death from the physical plane the disintegrating forces of Nature begin to operate upon his astral body, and this elemental thus finds his existence as a separate entity endangered. He sets to work therefore to defend himself, and to hold the astral body together as long as possible; and his method of doing this is to rearrange the matter of which it is composed in a sort of stratified series of shells, leaving that of the lowest (and therefore coarsest and grossest) sub-plane on the outside, since that will offer the greatest resistance to disintegration.

A man has to stay upon this lowest subdivision until he has disentangled so much as is possible of his true self from the matter of that sub-plane; and when that is done his consciousness is focused in the next of these concentric shells (that formed of the matter of the sixth subdivision), or to put the same idea in other words, he passes on to the next sub-plane. We might say that when the astral body has exhausted its attractions to one level, the greater part of its grosser particles fall away, and it finds itself in affinity with a somewhat higher state of existence. Its specific gravity, as it were, is constantly decreasing, and so it steadily rises from the denser to the lighter strata, pausing only when it is exactly balanced for a time.

This is evidently the explanation of a remark frequently made by the departed who appear at *séances* to the effect that they are about to rise to a higher sphere, from which it will be impossible, or not so easy, to communicate through a medium; and it is as a matter of fact true that a person upon the highest subdivision of this plane would find it almost impossible to deal with any ordinary medium.

Thus we see that the length of a man's detention upon any level of the astral plane will be precisely in proportion to the amount of its matter which is found in his astral body, and that in turn depends upon the life he has lived, the desires he has indulged, and the class of matter which by so doing he has attracted towards him and built into himself. It is, therefore, possible for a man, by pure living and high thinking, to minimize the quantity of matter belonging to the lower astral levels which he attaches to himself, and to raise it in each case to what may be called its critical point, so that the first touch of disintegrating force should shatter its cohesion and resolve it into its original condition, leaving him free at once to pass on to the next sub-plane.

In the case of a thoroughly spiritually-minded person this condition has been attained with reference to all the subdivisions of astral matter, and the result is a practically instantaneous passage through that plane, so that he recovers consciousness for the first time in the heaven-world. As was explained before, we never think of the sub-planes as being divided from one another in space, but rather as interpenetrating one another; so that when we say that a person passes from one subdivision to another, we do not necessarily mean that he moves in space at all, but that the focus of his consciousness shifts from the outer shell to that next within it.

The only persons who normally awake to consciousness on the lowest level of the astral plane are those whose desires are gross and brutal – drunkards, sensualists, and such like. There they remain for a period proportioned to the strength of their desires, often suffering terribly from the fact that while these earthly lusts are still as strong as ever, they now find it impossible to gratify them, except occasionally in a vicarious manner when they are able to seize upon some like-minded person, and obsess him.

The ordinarily decent man has little to detain him on that seventh sub-plane; but if his chief desires and thoughts had centred in more worldly affairs, he is likely to find himself in the sixth subdivision, still hovering about the places and persons with which he was most closely connected while on earth. The fifth and the fourth sub-planes are of similar character, except that as we rise through them mere earthly associations appear to become of less and less importance, and the departed tends more and more to mould his surroundings into agreements with the more persistent of his thoughts.

By the time we reach the third subdivision we find that this characteristic has entirely superseded the vision of the realities of the plane; for here the people are living in imaginary cities of their own – not each evolved entirely by his own thought, as in the heaven-world, but inheriting and adding to the structures erected by the thoughts of their predecessors. Here it is that the churches and schools and "dwellings in the summerland," so often described at spiritualistic *séances,* are to be found; though they often seem much less real and much less magnificent to an unprejudiced living observer than they are to their delighted creators.

The second sub-plane seems especially the habitat of the selfish or unspiritual religionist; here he wears his golden crown and worships his own grossly material representation of the particular deity of his country and time. The highest subdivision appears to be specially appropriate to those who during life have devoted themselves to materialistic but

33

intellectual pursuits, following them not for the sake of benefiting their fellowmen thereby, as from motives of selfish ambition or for the sake of intellectual exercise. Such persons will often remain upon this level for many long years – happy enough indeed in working out their intellectual problems, but doing no good to anyone, and making but little progress on their way towards the heaven-world.

It must be clearly understood, as before explained, that the idea of space is not in any way to be associated with these sub-planes. A departed entity functioning upon any one of them might drift with equal ease from England to Australia, or wherever a passing thought might take him; but he would not be able to transfer his consciousness from that sub-plane to the next above it until the process of detachment described had been completed.

To this rule there is no kind of exception, so far as we are yet aware, although naturally a man's actions when he finds himself conscious upon any sub-plane may within certain limits either shorten or prolong his connection with it.

But the amount of consciousness that a person has upon a given sub-plane does not invariably follow precisely the same law. Let us consider an extreme example of possible variation in order that we may grasp its method. Suppose a man who has brought over from his past incarnation tendencies requiring for their manifestation a very large amount of the matter of the seventh or lowest sub-plane, but has in his present life been fortunate enough to learn in his very earliest years the possibility and necessity of controlling these tendencies. It is scarcely probable that such a man's efforts at control should be entirely and uniformly successful; but if they were, the substitution of finer for grosser particles in his astral body would progress steadily, though slowly.

This process is at best gradual, and it might well happen that the man died before it was half completed. In that case there would undoubtedly be enough matter of the lowest sub-plane left in his astral body to ensure him no inconsiderable residence there; but it would be matter through which in this incarnation his consciousness had never been in the habit of functioning, and as it could not suddenly acquire this habit the result would be that the man would rest upon that sub-plane until his share of its matter was disintegrated but would be all the while in a condition of unconsciousness – that is to say, he would practically sleep through the period of his sojourn there, and so would be entirely unaffected by its many disagreeables.

The student of occultism, however, may make of his astral life something quite different from all this. The ordinary man, on awaking from the moment of unconsciousness which always seems to occur at death, finds himself in certain conditions which the desire-elemental has created for him by his rearrangement of the matter of the astral body. He can receive vibrations from without only through that type of matter which the elemental has left on the outside, and consequently his vision is limited to that particular sub-plane. The man accepts this limitation as part of the conditions of his new life; indeed he is quite unconscious that there is any limitation, and he supposes that what he sees is all that there is to see, since he knows nothing of the elemental or of its action.

The Theosophical student, however, understands all this, and therefore he knows that the limitation is not necessary. Knowing this he will at once set himself to resist the action of the desire-elemental, and will insist upon retaining his astral body in the same condition as during his earth-life – that is to say, with all its particles intermingled and in free motion. The consequence of this will be that he will be able to receive the vibrations from the matter of every astral sub-plane simultaneously, and so the whole astral world will be fully open to his sight. He will be able to move about in it just as freely as he could during physical sleep, and he can therefore find and communicate with any person in the astral plane, no matter to what subdivision that person may for the moment be confined.

The effort to resist the rearrangement, and restore the astral body to its former condition, is precisely similar to that which has to be made in resisting a strong desire during physical life. The elemental is afraid in his curious semi-conscious way, and he endeavours to transfer his fear to the man; so that the latter constantly finds a strong instinct creeping over him of some indescribable danger which can only be avoided by permitting the rearrangement. If, however, he steadily resists this unreasoning sense of dread by the calm assertion of his own knowledge that there is no cause for fear, he wears out in time the resistance of the elemental, just as he has resisted the prompting of desire many a time during his earthly life. Thus he becomes a living power during his astral life, able to carry on the work of helping others as he used to do during his hours of sleep.

It may be said in passing that communication is limited on the astral plane by the knowledge of the entity, just as it is here. While a pupil able to use his mind-body can communicate his thoughts to the human entities there present more readily and rapidly than on earth, by means of mental impressions, the inhabitants of the plane are not usually able to exercise this power, but appear to be restricted by limitations similar to those that prevail on earth, though perhaps less rigid. The result of this is that they are found associating there as here, in groups drawn together by common sympathies, belief, and language.

The poetic idea of death as a universal leveller is a mere absurdity born of ignorance, for, as a matter of fact, in the vast majority of cases the loss of the physical body makes no difference whatever in the character or intellect of the person, and there are therefore as many different varieties of intelligence among those whom we usually call the dead as among the living.

The popular religious teaching of the West as to man's *post-mortem* adventures has long been so wildly inaccurate that even intelligent people are often terribly puzzled when they recover consciousness in the astral world after death. The condition in which the new arrival finds himself differs so radically from what he has been led to expect that it is no uncommon case for him to refuse at first to believe that he has passed through the portals of death at all; indeed, of so little practical value is our much-vaunted belief in the

36

immortality of the soul that most people consider the very fact that they are still conscious an absolute proof that they have not died.

The horrible doctrine of eternal punishment, too, is responsible for a vast amount of most pitiable and entirely groundless terror among those newly arrived in this higher life. In many cases they spend long periods of acute mental suffering before they can free themselves from the fatal influence of that hideous blasphemy, and realize that the world is governed not according to the caprice of some demon who gloats over human anguish, but according to a benevolent and wonderfully patient law of evolution. Many members of the class we are considering do not really attain an intelligent appreciation of this fact of evolution at all, but drift through their astral interlude in the same aimless manner in which they have spent the physical portion of their lives. Thus after death, exactly as before it, there are the few who comprehend something of their position and know how to make the best of it, and the many who have not yet acquired that knowledge; and then, just as now, the ignorant are rarely ready to profit by the advice or example of the wise.

But of whatever grade the entity's intellect may be, it is always a fluctuating and on the whole a gradually diminishing quantity, for the lower mind of the man is being drawn in opposite directions by the higher spiritual nature which acts on it from above its level and the strong desire-forces which operate from below; and therefore it oscillates between the two attractions, with an ever increasing tendency towards the former as the forces of lower desire wear themselves out.

Here comes in one of the objections to the spiritualistic *séance.* An exceedingly ignorant or degraded man may no doubt learn much by coming into contact after his death with a circle of earnest sitters under the control of some reliable person, and so may be really helped and raised. But in the ordinary man the consciousness is steadily rising from the lower part of the nature towards the higher; and obviously it cannot be helpful to his evolution that this lower part should be reawakened from the natural and desirable unconsciousness into which it is passing, and dragged back into touch with earth in order to communicate through a medium.

The peculiar danger of this will be seen when it is recollected that since the real man is all the while steadily withdrawing into himself, he is as time goes on less and less able to influence or guide this lower portion, which nevertheless, until the separation is complete, has the power to generate karma, and under the circumstances is evidently far more likely to add evil than good to its record.

Apart altogether from any question of development through a medium, there is another and much more frequently exercised influence which may seriously retard a disembodied entity on his way to the heaven-world, and that is the intense and uncontrolled grief of his surviving friends or relatives. It is one among many melancholy results of the terribly inaccurate and even irreligious view that we in the West have for centuries been taking of death, that we not only cause ourselves an immense amount of wholly unnecessary pain over this temporary parting from our loved ones, but we often also do serious injury to those for whom we bear so deep an affection by means of this very regret which we feel so acutely.

When our departed brother is sinking peacefully and naturally into the unconsciousness which precedes his awakening amid the glories of the heaven-world, he is too frequently aroused from his dreamy happiness into vivid remembrance of the earth-life which he has lately left, solely by the action of the passionate sorrows and desires of his friends on earth, which awaken corresponding vibrations in his own desire-body, and so cause him acute discomfort.

It would be well if those whose comrades have passed on before them would learn from these undoubted facts the duty of restraining for the sake of those friends a grief which, however natural it may be, is yet in its essence selfish. Not that occult teaching counsels forgetfulness of the dead – far from it; but it does suggest that a man's affectionate remembrance of his departed friend is a force which, if properly directed into the channel of earnest good wishes for his progress towards the heaven-world and his quiet passage through the intermediate state, might be of real value to him, whereas when wasted in mourning for him and longing to have him back again it is not only useless but harmful. It is with a true instinct that the Hindu religion prescribes its Shraddha ceremonies and the Catholic Church its prayers for the dead.

It sometimes happens, however, that the desire for communication is from the other side, and that the dead man has something, which he specially desires to say to those whom he has left behind. Occasionally this message is an important one, such as, for example, an indication of the place where a missing will is concealed; but more often it seems to us quite trivial. Still, whatever it may be, if it is firmly impressed upon the mind of the dead person, it is undoubtedly desirable that he should be enabled to deliver it, as otherwise the anxiety to do so would perpetually draw his consciousness back into the earth-life, and prevent him from passing to higher spheres. In such a case a psychic who can understand him, or a medium through whom he can write or speak, is of real service to him.

Why cannot he write or speak without a medium? It may be asked. The reason is that one state of matter can ordinarily act only upon the state next below it, and, as he has now no denser matter in his organism than that of which the astral body is composed, he finds it impossible to set up vibrations in the physical substance of the air or to move the physical pencil without borrowing living matter of the intermediate order contained in the etheric double, by means of which an impulse can readily be transferred from the one plane to the other. He is unable to borrow this material from an ordinary person, because such a man's principles would be too closely linked together to be separated by any means likely to be at his command, but the very essence of mediumship is the ready separability of the principles, so from a medium he can draw without difficulty the matter he needs for his manifestation, whatever it may be.

When he cannot find a medium or does not understand how to use one he sometimes makes clumsy and blundering endeavours to communicate on his own account, and by the strength of his will he sets elemental forces blindly working, perhaps producing such apparently aimless manifestations as stone-throwing, bell-ringing, etc. It consequently frequently happens that a psychic or medium going to a house where such manifestations are taking place may be able to discover what the entity who produces them is attempting to say or do, and may thus put an end to the disturbance. This would not, however, invariably be the case, as these elemental forces are occasionally set in motion by entirely different causes.

4. *The Shade.* When the separation of the principles is complete, the astral life of the person is over, and, as before stated, he passes into the mental condition. But just as when he dies to this plane he leaves his physical body behind him, so when he dies to the astral plane he leaves a disintegrating astral body behind him. If he has purged himself from all earthly desires during life, and directed all his energies into the channels of unselfish spiritual aspiration, the higher ego will be able to draw back into itself the whole of the lower mind which he put forth into incarnation; in that case the body left behind on the astral plane will be a mere corpse like the abandoned physical body, and it will then come not into this class but into the next.

Even in the case of a man of somewhat less perfect life almost the same result may be attained if the forces of lower desire are allowed to work themselves out undisturbed in the astral plane. But the majority of mankind make but trifling and perfunctory efforts while on earth to rid themselves of the less elevated impulses of their nature, and consequently doom themselves not only to a greatly prolonged sojourn in the intermediate world, but also to what cannot be described otherwise than as a loss of a portion of the lower mind.

This is, no doubt, a material method of expressing the reflection of the higher manas in the lower, but a very fairly accurate idea of what actually takes place will be obtained by adopting the hypothesis that the manasic principle sends down a portion of itself into the lower world of physical life at each incarnation, and expects to be able to withdraw it again at the end of the life, enriched by all its varied experiences. The ordinary man, however, usually allows himself to be so pitiably enslaved by all sorts of base desires that a certain portion of this lower mind becomes closely interwoven with the desire-body, and when the separation takes place at the close of his astral life the mental principle has, as it were, to be torn apart, the degraded portion remaining within the disintegrating astral body.

This body then consists of the particles of astral matter from which the lower mind has not been able to disengage itself, which therefore retain it captive; for when the man passes into the heaven-world these clinging fragments adhere to a portion of his mind, and as it were wrench it away. The proportion of the matter of each level present in the decaying astral vehicle will therefore depend on the extent to which the mind has become inextricably entangled with the lower passions. It will be obvious that as the mind in passing from level to level is unable to free itself completely from the matter of each, the astral remnant will show the presence of each grosser kind, which has succeeded in retaining its connection with it.

Thus comes into existence the class of entity which has been called "The Shade" – an entity, be it observed, which is not in any sense the real individual at all, for *he* has passed away into the heaven-world; but nevertheless, it not only bears his exact personal appearance, but possesses his memory and all his little idiosyncrasies, and may therefore readily be mistaken for him, as indeed it frequently is at *séances*. It is not conscious of any act of impersonation, for as far as its intellect goes it must necessarily suppose itself to be the individual, but one can imagine the horror and disgust of the friends of the departed, if they could only realize that they had been deceived into accepting as their comrade a mere soulless bundle of all his lowest qualities.

The length of life of a shade varies according to the amount of the lower mind which animates it, but as this is all the while in process of fading out, its intellect is a steadily diminishing quantity, though it may possess a great deal of a certain sort of animal cunning; and even quite towards the end of its career it is still able to communicate by borrowing temporary intelligence from the medium. From its nature it is exceedingly liable to be swayed by all kinds of evil influences and, having separated from its ego, it has nothing in its constitution capable of responding to anything higher. It therefore lends itself readily to various minor purposes of some of the baser sort of black magicians. So much of mental matter as it possesses gradually disintegrates and returns to its own plane, though not to any individual mind, and thus the shade fades by almost imperceptible gradations into a member of our next class.

5. *The Shell.* This is absolutely the mere astral corpse in the later stages of its disintegration, every particle of the mind having left it. It is entirely without any kind of consciousness or intelligence and drifts passively about upon the astral currents just as a cloud might be swept in any direction by a passing breeze; but even yet it may be galvanized for a few moments into a ghastly burlesque of life if it happens to come within reach of a medium's aura. Under such circumstances it still exactly resembles its departed personality in appearance, and may even reproduce to some extent his familiar expressions or handwriting, but it does so merely by the automatic action of the cells of which it is composed, which tend under stimulation to repeat the form of action to which they are most accustomed. Whatever amount of intelligence may lie behind any such manifestation has no connection with the original man, but is lent by the medium or his "guides" for the occasion.

It is, however, more frequently temporarily vitalized in quite another manner, which will be described under the next head. It has also the quality of being still blindly responsive to such vibrations – usually of the lowest order – as were frequently set up in it during its last stage of existence as a shade, and consequently persons in whom evil desires or passions are predominant will be likely, if they attend physical *séances,* to find these intensified and as it were thrown back upon them by the unconscious shells.

There is also another variety of corpse which it is necessary to mention under this head, though it belongs to a much earlier stage of man's *post-mortem* history. It has been stated above that after the death of the physical body the astral vehicle is comparatively quickly rearranged, and the etheric double cast off – this latter body being destined to slow disintegration, precisely as is the astral shell at a later stage of the proceedings.

This etheric shell, however, does not drift aimlessly about, as does the variety with which we have hitherto been dealing; on the contrary, it remains within a few yards of the decaying physical body, and since it is readily visible to any one even slightly sensitive, it accounts for many of the commonly current stories of church-yard ghosts. A psychically developed person passing one of our great cemeteries may see many of these bluish-white, misty forms hovering over the graves where are laid the physical vestures which they have recently left; and as they, like their lower counterparts, are in stages of disintegration, the sight is by no means pleasant.

This also, like the other kind of shell, is entirely devoid of consciousness and intelligence; and though it may under certain circumstances be galvanized into a horrible form of temporary life, this is possible only by means of some of the most loathsome rites of one of the worst forms of black magic, about which the less said the better. It will thus be seen that in the successive stages of his progress from earth-life to the heaven-world, man casts off and leaves to slow disintegration no less than three corpses – the dense physical body, the etheric double, and the astral vehicle – all of which are by degrees resolved into their constituent elements and their matter utilized anew on their respective planes by the wonderful chemistry of Nature.

6. *The Vitalized Shell.* This entity ought not, strictly speaking, to be classified under the head "human" at all, since it is only its outer vesture, the passive, senseless shell, that was once an appanage of humanity; such life, intelligence, desire, and will as it may possess are those of the artificial-elemental animating it, and that, though in truth a creation of man's evil thought is not itself human. It will therefore perhaps be better to deal with it more fully under its appropriate class among the artificial entities, as its nature and genesis will be more readily comprehensible by the time that part of our subject is reached.

Let it suffice here to mention that it is always a malevolent being – a true tempting demon, whose evil influence is limited only by the extent of its power. Like the shade, it is frequently used to further the horrible purposes of the Voodoo and Obeah and other forms of Black magic. Some writers have spoken of it under the name "elementary," but as that title has at one time or another been used for almost every variety of *post-mortem* entity, it has become so vague and meaningless that it is perhaps better to avoid it.

7. *The Suicide and the victim of sudden death.* It will be readily understood that a man who is torn from physical life hurriedly while in full health and strength, whether by accident or suicide, finds himself upon the astral plane under conditions differing considerably from those which surround one who dies either from old age or from disease. In the latter case the hold of earthly desires upon the entity is sure to be more or less weakened, and probably the very grossest particles are already eliminated, so that the man is likely to find himself on the sixth or fifth subdivision of the astral world, or perhaps even higher; the principles have been gradually prepared for separation, and the shock is therefore not so great.

In the case of the accidental death or suicide none of these preparations have taken place, and the withdrawal of the principles from their physical encasement has been aptly compared to the tearing of the stone out of an unripe fruit; much of the grossest kind of astral matter may still cling round the personality, which will consequently be held in the seventh or lowest subdivision of the plane. This has already been described as anything but a pleasant abiding-place, yet it is by no means the same for all those who are compelled for a time to inhabit it. Those victims of sudden death whose earth-lives have been pure and noble have no affinity for this plane, and so the time of their sojourn upon it is passed, to quote from an early letter on this subject, either in "happy ignorance and full oblivion, or in a state of quiet slumber, a sleep full of rosy dreams."

On the other hand, if men's earth-lives have been low and brutal, selfish and sensual, they will be conscious to the fullest extent in this undesirable region; and it is possible for them to develop into terribly evil entities. Inflamed with all kinds of horrible appetites which they call no longer satisfy directly now they are without a physical body, they gratify their loathsome passions vicariously through a medium or any sensitive person whom they can obsess; and they take a devilish delight in using all the arts of delusion which the astral plane puts in their power in order to lead others into the same excesses which have proved so fatal to themselves.

Quoting again from the same letter: "These are the Pisachas, the *incubi* and *succubæ* of mediæval writers – demons of thirst and gluttony, of lust and avarice, of intensified craft, wickedness, and cruelty, provoking their victims to horrible crimes, and reveling in their commission." From this class and the last are drawn the tempters – the devils of ecclesiastical literature; but their power falls utterly before purity of mind and purpose; they can do nothing with a man unless he has first encouraged in himself the vices into which they seek to draw him.

One whose psychic sight has been opened will often see crowds of these unfortunate creatures hanging round butchers' shops, public-houses, or other even more disreputable places – wherever the gross influences in which they delight are to be found, and where they encounter men and women still in the flesh who are likeminded with themselves. For such an entity as one of these to meet with a medium with whom he is in affinity is indeed a terrible misfortune; not only does it enable him to prolong enormously his dreadful astral life, but it renews for perhaps an indefinite period his power to generate evil karma, and so prepare for himself a future incarnation of the most degraded character, besides running the risk of losing a large portion of such mind-power as he may happen to possess. If he is fortunate enough *not* to meet with a sensitive through whom his passions can be vicariously gratified, the unfulfilled desires will gradually burn themselves out, and the suffering caused in the process will probably go far towards working off the evil karma of the past life.

The position of the suicide is further complicated by the fact that his rash act has diminished the power of the ego to withdraw its lower portion into itself, and therefore has exposed him to various additional dangers; but it must be remembered that the guilt of suicide differs considerably according to its circumstances, from the morally blameless act of Seneca or Socrates through all degrees down to the heinous crime of the wretch who takes his own life in order to escape from the entanglements into which his villainy has brought him; and the position after death varies accordingly.

It should be noted that this class, as well as the shades and the vitalized shells are all what may be called minor vampires; that is to say, whenever they have the opportunity they prolong their existence by draining away the vitality from human beings whom they find themselves able to influence. This is why both medium and sitters are often so weak and exhausted after a physical *séance*. A student of occultism is taught how to guard himself from their attempts, but without that knowledge it is difficult for one who puts himself in their way to avoid being more or less laid under contribution by them.

8. *The Vampire and Werewolf.* There remain two even more vile but happily rare possibilities to be mentioned before this part of our subject is completed, and though they differ widely in many ways we may yet perhaps group them together, since they have in common the qualities of unearthly horror and of extreme rarity – the latter arising from the fact that they are really legacies from earlier races – hideous anachronisms, appalling relics of a time when man and his surroundings were in many ways not what they are now.

We of the fifth root race ought to have evolved beyond the possibility of meeting such a ghastly fate as is indicated by either of the two headings of this sub-section, and we have so nearly done it that these creatures are commonly regarded as mere mediaeval fables; yet there *are* examples to be found occasionally even now. The popular legends about them are probably often considerably exaggerated, but there is nevertheless a terribly serious substratum of truth beneath the eerie stories, which pass from mouth to mouth among the peasantry of Eastern Europe. The general characteristics of such tales are too well known to need more than a passing reference; a fairly typical specimen of the vampire story, though it does not profess to be more than the merest fiction, is Sheridan le Fanu's *Carmilla,* while a very remarkable account of an unusual form of this creature is to be found in *Isis Unveiled.*

Readers of Theosophical literature will be aware that it is just possible for a man to live a life so absolutely degraded and selfish, so utterly wicked and brutal, that the whole of his lower mind may become entirely enmeshed in his desires, and finally separate from its spiritual source in the higher self. Some students even seem to have supposed that such an occurrence is quite common, and that we may meet scores of such "soulless men", as they have been called, in the street every day of our lives; but this, happily, is untrue. To attain the appalling pre-eminence in evil which thus involves the entire loss of a personality and the weakening of the developing individuality behind, a man must stifle every gleam of unselfishness or spirituality, and must have absolutely no redeeming point whatever; and when we remember how often, even in the worst of villains, there is to be found something not wholly bad, we shall realize that the abandoned personalities must always be a very small minority. Still, comparatively few though they be, they do exist, and it is from their ranks that the still rarer vampire is drawn.

The lost entity would very soon after death find himself unable to stay in the astral world, and would be irresistibly drawn in full consciousness into "his own place", the mysterious eighth sphere, there slowly to disintegrate after experiences best left undescribed. If, however, he perishes by suicide or sudden death, he may under certain circumstances, especially if he knows something of black magic, hold himself back from that appalling fate by a death in life scarcely less appalling – the ghastly existence of the vampire.

Since the eighth sphere cannot claim him until after the death of the body, he preserves it in a kind of cataleptic trance by the horrible expedient of the transfusion into it of blood drawn from other human beings by his semi-materialized astral, and thus postpones his final destiny by the commission of wholesale murder. As popular "superstition" again rightly supposes, the easiest and most effectual remedy in such a case is to exhume and burn the body, thus depriving the creature of his *point d' appui.* When the grave is opened the body usually appears quite fresh and healthy, and the coffin is not infrequently filled with blood. In countries where cremation is the custom, vampirism of this sort is naturally impossible.

The Werewolf, though equally horrible, is the product of a somewhat different karma, and indeed ought perhaps to have found a place under the first instead of the second division of the human inhabitants of this plane, since it is always during a man's lifetime that he first manifests under this form. It invariably implies some knowledge of magical arts – sufficient at any rate to be able to project the astral body.

When a perfectly cruel and brutal man does this, there are certain circumstances under which the body may be seized upon by other astral entities and materialized, not into the human form, but into that of some wild animal – usually the wolf; and in that condition it will range the surrounding country killing other animals, and even human beings, thus satisfying not only its own craving for blood, but that of the fiends who drive it on.

In this case, as so often with ordinary materialization, any wound inflicted upon that animal form will be reproduced upon the human physical body by the extraordinary phenomenon of repercussion; though after the death of that physical body, the astral (which will probably continue to appear in the same form) will be less vulnerable. It will then, however, be also less dangerous, as unless it can find a suitable medium it will be unable to materialize fully. In such manifestations there is probably a great deal of the matter of the etheric double, and perhaps also a toll is levied upon the gaseous and liquid constituents of the physical body, as in the case of some materializations. In both cases the fluidic body appears able to pass to much greater distances from the physical than is ever otherwise possible, so far as is yet known, for a vehicle, which contains at least a certain amount of etheric matter.

It has been the fashion of this age to scoff at what are called the foolish superstitions of the ignorant peasantry; but as in the above cases, so in many others, the occult student finds on careful examination that obscure or forgotten truths of Nature lie behind what at first sight appears mere nonsense, and he learns to be cautious in rejecting as well as cautious in accepting. Intending explorers of the astral plane need have little fear of encountering the very unpleasant creatures described under this head, for, as before stated, they are even now extremely rare, and as time goes on their number will happily steadily diminish. In any case their manifestations are usually restricted to the immediate neighbourhood of their physical bodies, as might be supposed from their extremely material nature.

9. *The Man in the Grey World.* I have already explained that the vampire and the werewolf are anachronisms, that they belonged to the evolution of an earlier root-race. But though we have developed beyond that particular form of manifestation of it, the type of person who clings desperately to physical life because he has no certainty that there is any other still persists among us. Having been intensely material, having had no ideas, no conceptions of any sort beyond the physical during earth-life, he becomes crazy with fear when he finds himself altogether cut adrift from it.

Sometimes such men make frantic efforts to return into some sort of touch with physical life. Most do not succeed, and gradually give up the struggle; as soon as they do that, they slip off at once into the natural moment of unconsciousness and shortly awaken in the astral world. But those, whose will is strong enough to attain a partial and temporary success hold on tenaciously to at least some fragments of their etheric double, and sometimes even manage to draw particles from their physical bodies.

We may say that the actual definition of death is the full and final separation of the etheric double from the dense body – or, to put it in other words, the breaking up of the physical body by withdrawing its etheric part from its lower part. So long as a link is maintained we may have conditions of catalepsy, trance or anaesthesia; when the link is finally broken, death has taken place.

When a man withdraws from his dense body at death, then, he takes with him the etheric part of that vehicle. But that etheric matter is not in itself a complete vehicle – only part of one. Therefore while that etheric matter still clings round him, he is neither on one plane nor the other. He has lost the organs of his physical senses, and he cannot use those of the astral body because he is still enveloped in this cloud of etheric matter. He lives for awhile – fortunately only for awhile – in a dim grey world of restlessness and discomfort, in which he can see clearly neither physical nor astral happenings, but catches occasional glimpses of both as through a world of heavy fog, in which he wanders, lost and helpless.

There is no reason whatever why any human being should suffer such unpleasantness at all; but he fears that in letting go that shred of consciousness he may lose all consciousness for ever – may in fact be annihilated; so he grasps desperately at this which is left to him. In time, however, he must let go, for the etheric double begins to disintegrate, and then he slips quite happily into the fuller and wider life.

Such people may sometimes be found drifting miserably and even wailingly about the astral plane, and it is one of the hardest tasks of the helper to persuade them that they have nothing to do but to forget their fear, to relax their tenseness, and to let themselves sink gently into the peace and oblivion which they need so sorely. They seem to regard such a suggestion as a ship-wrecked man far away from land might receive an order to abandon his supporting spar, and trust himself to the stormy sea.

10. *The Black Magician or his pupil.* This person corresponds at the other extremity of the scale to our second class of departed entities, the pupil awaiting reincarnation, but in this case, instead of obtaining permission to adopt an unusual method of progress, the man is defying the natural process of evolution by maintaining himself in astral life by magical arts – sometimes of the most horrible nature.

It would be easy to make various subdivisions of this class, according to their objects, their methods, and the possible duration of their existence on this plane, but as they are by no means fascinating objects of study, and all that in occult student wishes to know about them is how to avoid them, it will probably be more interesting to pass on to the examination of another part of our subject. It may, however, be just mentioned that every such human entity which prolongs its life thus on the astral plane beyond its natural limit invariably does so at the expense of others, and by the absorption of their life in some form or another.

II. NON-HUMAN

It might have been thought fairly obvious, even to the most casual glance, that many of the terrestrial arrangements of Nature which affect us most nearly have not been designed exclusively with a view to our comfort, to even our ultimate advantage. Yet it was probably unavoidable that the human race, at least in its childhood, should imagine that this world and everything it contains existed solely for its own use and benefit; but undoubtedly we ought by this time to have grown out of that infantile delusion and realized our proper position and the duties that attach to it.

That most of us have not yet done so is shown in a dozen ways in our daily life – notably by the atrocious cruelty habitually displayed towards the animal kingdom under the name of sport by many who probably consider themselves highly civilized people. The veriest tyro in the holy science of occultism knows that all life is sacred and that without universal compassion there is no true progress; but it is only as he advances in his studies that he discovers how manifold evolution is, and how comparatively small a place humanity really fills in the economy of Nature.

It becomes clear to him that as earth, air, and water support myriads of forms of life which, though invisible to the ordinary eye, are revealed to us by the microscope, so the higher planes connected with our earth have an equally dense population of whose existence we are ordinarily completely unconscious. As his knowledge increases he becomes more and more certain that in one way or another the utmost use is being made of every possibility of evolution, and that wherever it seems to us that in Nature force is being wasted or opportunity neglected, it is not the scheme of the universe that is in fault, but our ignorance of its method and intention.

For the purposes of our present consideration of the non-human inhabitants of the astral plane it will be best to leave altogether out of consideration those early forms of the universal life which are evolving, in a manner of which we can have little comprehension, through the successive encasement of atoms, molecules, and cells. If we commence at the lowest of what are usually called the elemental kingdoms, we shall even then have to group together under this general heading an enormous number of inhabitants of the astral plane upon whom it will be possible to touch only slightly, as anything like a detailed account of them would swell this manual to the dimensions of an encyclopaedia.

The most convenient method of arranging the non-human entities will perhaps be in four classes – it being understood that in this case the class is not, as previously, a comparatively small subdivision, but usually a great kingdom of Nature at least as large and varied as, say, the animal or vegetable kingdom. Some of these classes rank considerably below humanity, some are our equals, and others again rise far above us in goodness and power. Some belong to our scheme of evolution – that is to say, they either have been or will be men like ourselves; others are evolving on entirely distinct lines of their own.

Before proceeding to consider them it is necessary in order to avoid the charge of incompleteness, to mention that in this branch of the subject two reservations have been made. First, no reference is made to the occasional appearances of high Adepts from other planets of the solar system and of even more august Visitors from a still greater distance, since such matters cannot fitly be described in an essay for general reading; and besides it is practically inconceivable, though theoretically possible, that such glorified Beings should ever need to manifest themselves on a plane so low as the astral. If for any reason they should wish to do so, the body appropriate to the plane would be temporarily created out of astral matter belonging to this planet, as in the case of the Nirmanakaya.

Secondly, quite outside of and entirely unconnected with the four classes into which we are dividing this section, there are two other great evolutions which at present share the use of this planet with humanity; but about them it is forbidden to give any particulars at this stage of the proceedings, as it is not apparently intended under ordinary circumstances either that they should be conscious of man's existence or man of theirs. If we ever do come into contact with them it will most probably be on the purely physical plane, for in any case their connection with our astral plane is of the slightest since the only possibility of their appearance there depends upon an extremely improbable accident in an act of ceremonial magic, which fortunately only a few of the most advanced sorcerers know how to perform. Nevertheless, that improbable accident has happened at least once, and may happen again, so that but for the prohibition above mentioned it would have been necessary to include them in our list.

1. *The Elemental Essence belonging to our own evolution.* As the name "elementary" has been given indiscriminately by various writers to any or all of man's possible *post-mortem* conditions, so this word "elemental" has been used at different times to mean any or all non-human spirits, from the most god-like of the Devas down through every variety of nature-spirit to the formless essence which pervades the kingdoms lying behind the mineral, until after reading several books the student becomes absolutely bewildered by the contradictory statements made on the subject. For the purposes of this treatise let it be understood that elemental essence is merely a name applied during certain stages of its evolution to monadic essence, which in its turn may be defined as the outpouring of Spirit or Divine Force into matter.

We are all familiar with the idea that before this outpouring arrives at the stage of individualization at which it forms the causal body of man, it has passed through and ensouled in turn six lower phases of evolution – the animal, vegetable, mineral, and three elemental kingdoms. When energizing through those respective stages it has sometimes been called the animal, vegetable, or mineral monad – though this term is distinctly misleading, since long before it arrives at any of these kingdoms it has become not *one*, but *many* monads. The name was, however, adopted to convey the idea that, though differentiation in the monadic essence had already long ago set in, it had not yet been carried to the extent of individualization.

When this monadic essence is energizing through the three great elemental kingdoms which precede the mineral, it is called by the name of "elemental essence." Before, however, its nature and the manner in which it manifests can be understood, the method in which spirit enfolds itself in its descent into matter must be realized.

Be it remembered, then, that when spirit resting on any plane (it matters not which – let us call it plane No. 1) wills to descend to the plane next below (let us call that plane No. 2) it must enfold itself in the matter of that plane – that is to say, it must draw round itself a veil of the matter of plane No. 2. Similarly when it continues its descent to plane No. 3, it must draw round itself the matter of that plane, and we shall then have, say, an atom whose body or outer covering consists of the matter of plane No. 3. The force energizing in it – its soul, so to speak – will however not be spirit in the condition in which it was on plane No. 1, but will be that divine force *plus* the veil of the matter of plane No. 2. When a still further descent is made to plane No. 4, the atom becomes still more complex, for it will then have a body of No. 4 matter, ensouled by spirit already twice veiled – in the matter of planes 2 and 3. It will be seen that, since this process repeats itself for every sub-plane of each plane of the solar system, by the time the original force reaches our physical level it is so thoroughly veiled that it is small wonder men often fail to recognize it as spirit at all.

Suppose that the monadic essence has carried on this process of veiling itself down to the atomic level of the mental plane, and that, instead of descending through the various subdivisions of that plane, it plunges down directly into the astral plane, ensouling, or aggregating round it a body of atomic astral matter; such a combination would be the elemental essence of the astral plane, belonging to the third of the great elemental kingdoms – that immediately preceding the mineral. In the course of its 2,401 differentiations on the astral plane it draws to itself many and various combinations of the matter of its several sub-divisions; but these are only temporary, and it still remains essentially one kingdom, whose characteristic is monadic essence involved down to the atomic level of the mental plane only, but manifesting through the atomic matter of the astral plane.

The two higher elemental kingdoms exist and function respectively upon the higher and the lower levels of the mental plane; but we are not at the moment concerned with them.

To speak, as we so often do, of *an* elemental in connection with the group we are now considering is somewhat misleading, for strictly speaking there is no such thing. What we find is a vast store of elemental essence, wonderfully sensitive to the most fleeting human thought, responding with inconceivable delicacy in an infinitesimal fraction of a second to a vibration set up in it even by an entirely unconscious exercise of human will or desire.

But the moment that by the influence of such thought or exercise of will it is moulded into a living force – into something that may correctly be described as *an* elemental – it at once ceases to belong to the category we are discussing, and becomes a member of the artificial class. Even then its separate existence is usually of the most evanescent character, and as soon as its impulse has worked itself out it sinks back into the undifferentiated mass of that particular subdivision of elemental essence from which it came.

It would be tedious to attempt to catalogue these subdivisions, and indeed even if a list of them were made it would be unintelligible except to the practical student who can call them up before him and compare them. Some idea of the leading lines of classification can, however, be grasped without much trouble, and may prove of interest.

First comes the broad division, which has given the elementals their name – the classification according to the kind of matter which they inhabit. Here, as usual, the septenary character of our evolution shows itself, for there are seven such chief groups, related respectively to the seven states of physical matter – to "earth, water, air, and fire," or to translate from mediæval symbolism to modern accuracy of expression, to the solid, the liquid, the gaseous, and the four etheric conditions.

It has long been the custom to pity and despise the ignorance of the alchemists of the middle ages, because they gave the title of "elements" to substances which modern chemistry has discovered to be compounds; but in speaking of them thus slightingly we have done them great injustice, for their knowledge on this subject was really wider, not narrower, than ours. They may or may not have catalogued all the eighty or ninety substances which we now call elements; but they certainly did not apply that name to them, for their occult studies had taught them that in that sense of the word there was but *one* element, of which these and all other forms of matter were but modifications – a truth which some of the greatest chemists of the present day are just beginning to suspect.

The fact is that in this particular case our despised forefathers' analysis went several steps deeper than our own. They understood and were able to observe the ether, which modern science can only postulate as a necessity for its theories; they were aware that it consists of physical matter in four entirely distinct states above the gaseous – a fact which has not yet been re-discovered. They knew that all physical objects consist of matter in one or other of these seven states, and that into the composition of every organic body all seven enter in a greater or lesser degree; hence all their talk of fiery and watery humours, or "elements," which seems so grotesque to us. It is obvious that they used the latter word as a synonym for "constituent parts," without in the least degree intending it to connote the idea of substances which could not be further reduced. They knew also that each of these orders of matter serves as a basis of manifestation for a great class of evolving monadic essence, and so they christened the essence "elemental."

What we have to try to realize, then, is that in every particle of solid matter, so long as it remains in that condition, there resides, to use the picturesque phraseology of mediæval students, an earth elemental – that is, a certain amount of the living elemental essence appropriate to it, while equally in every particle of matter in the liquid, gaseous, or etheric states, the water, air, and fire "elementals" respectively inhere. It will be observed that this first broad division of the third of the elemental kingdoms is, so to speak, horizontal – that is to say, its respective classes stand in the relation of steps, each somewhat less material than that below it, which ascends into it by almost imperceptible degrees; and it is easy to understand how each of these classes may again he divided horizontally into seven, since there are obviously many degrees of density among solids, liquids, and gases.

There is, however, what may be described as a perpendicular division also, and this is somewhat more difficult to comprehend, especially as great reserve is always maintained by occultists as to some of the facts which would be involved in a fuller explanation of it. Perhaps the clearest way to put what is known on the subject will be to state that in each of the horizontal classes and subclasses will be found seven perfectly distinct types of elemental, the difference between them being no longer a question of degree of materiality, but rather of character and affinities.

Each of these types so reacts upon the others that, though it is impossible for them ever to interchange their essence, in each of them seven sub-types will be found to exist, distinguished by the colouring given to their original peculiarity by the influence which sways them most readily. It will be seen that this perpendicular division and subdivision differs entirely in its character from the horizontal, in that it is far more permanent and fundamental; for while it is the evolution of the elemental kingdom to pass with almost infinite slowness through its various horizontal classes and sub-classes in succession, and thus to belong to them all in turn, this is not so with regard to the types and sub-types, which remain unchangeable all the way through.

A point of which we must never lose sight in endeavouring to understand this elemental evolution is that it is taking place on what is sometimes called the downward curve of the arc; that is to say, it is progressing *towards* the complete entanglement in matter which we witness in the mineral kingdom, instead of *away* from it, as is most other evolution of which we know anything. Thus for it progress means descent into matter instead of ascent towards higher planes; and this fact sometimes gives it a curiously inverted appearance in our eyes until we thoroughly grasp its object. Unless the student bears this constantly and clearly in mind, he will again and again find himself beset by perplexing anomalies.

In spite of these manifold subdivisions, there are certain properties which are possessed in common by all varieties of this strange living essence; but even these are so entirely different from any with which we are familiar on the physical plane that it is exceedingly difficult to explain them to those who cannot themselves see them in action.

Let it be premised, then, that when any portion of this essence remains for a few moments entirely unaffected by any outside influence (a condition, by the way, which is hardly ever realized) it is absolutely without any definite form of its own, though its motion is still rapid and ceaseless; but on the slightest disturbance, set up perhaps by some passing thought-current, it flashes into a bewildering confusion of restless, ever-changing shapes, which form, rush about, and disappear with the rapidity of the bubbles on the surface of boiling water.

These evanescent shapes, though generally those of living creatures of some sort, human or otherwise, no more express the existence of separate entities in the essence than do the equally changeful and multiform waves raised in a few moments on a previously smooth lake by a sudden squall. They seem to be mere reflections from the vast storehouse of the astral plane, yet they have usually a certain appropriateness to the character of the thought stream, which calls them into existence, though nearly always with some grotesque distortion, some terrifying or unpleasant aspect about them.

A question naturally arises in the mind here as to what intelligence it is that is exerted in the selection of an appropriate shape or its distortion when selected. We are not dealing with the more powerful and longer-lived artificial elemental created by a strong definite thought, but with the result produced by the stream of half conscious, involuntary thoughts which the majority of mankind allow to flow idly through their brains. The intelligence, therefore, is obviously not derived from the mind of the thinker; and we certainly cannot credit the elemental essence itself, which belongs to a kingdom further from individualization even than the mineral, with any sort of awakening of the mental quality.

Yet it does possess a marvellous adaptability which often seems to come near it, and it is no doubt this property that caused elementals to be described in one of our early books as "the semi-intelligent creatures of the astral light." We shall find further evidence of this power when we come to consider the case of the artificial class. When we read of a good or evil elemental, it must always be either an artificial entity or one of the many varieties of nature-spirits that is meant, for the elemental kingdoms proper do not admit of any such conceptions as good and evil.

There is, however, undoubtedly a sort of bias or tendency permeating nearly all their subdivisions, which operates to render them rather hostile than friendly towards man. Every neophyte knows this, for in most cases his very first impression of the astral plane is of the presence all around him of vast hosts of protean spectres who advance upon him in threatening guise, but always retire or dissipate harmlessly if boldly faced. It is to this curious tendency that the distorted or unpleasant aspect above mentioned must be referred, and mediæval writers tell us that man has only himself to thank for its existence. In the golden age before this sordid present, men were on the whole less selfish and more spiritual, and then the "elementals" were friendly, though now they are so no longer because of man's indifference to, and want of sympathy with, other living beings.

From the wonderful delicacy with which the essence responds to the faintest action of our minds or desires, it seems clear that this elemental kingdom as a whole is much what the collective thought of humanity makes it. Any one who will think for a moment how far from elevating the action of that collective thought is likely to be at the present time, will see little reason to wonder that we reap as we have sown, and that this essence, which has no power of perception, but only blindly receives and reflects what is projected upon it, should usually exhibit unfriendly characteristics.

There can be no doubt that in later races or rounds, when mankind as a whole has evolved to a much higher level, the elemental kingdoms will be influenced by the changed thought which continually impinges upon them, and we shall find them no longer hostile, but docile and helpful as we are told that the animal kingdom will also be. Whatever may have happened in the past, it is evident that we may look forward to a passable "golden age" in the future, if we can arrive at a time when the majority of men will be noble and unselfish, and the forces of nature will co-operate willingly with them.

The fact that we are so readily able to influence the elemental kingdoms shows us that we have a responsibility towards them for the manner in which we use that influence. Indeed, when we consider the conditions under which they exist, it is obvious that the effect produced upon them by the thoughts and desires of all intelligent creatures inhabiting the same world with them must have been calculated upon in the scheme of our system as a factor in their evolution.

In spite of the consistent teaching of all the great religions, the mass of mankind is still utterly regardless of its responsibility on the thought-plane; if a man can flatter himself that his words and deeds have been harmless to others, he believes that he has done all that can be required of him, quite oblivious of the fact that he may for years have been exercising a narrowing and debasing influence on the minds of those about him, and filling surrounding space with the unlovely creations of a sordid mind. A still more serious aspect of this question will come before us when we discuss the artificial elemental; but in regard to the essence it will be sufficient to state that we undoubtedly have the power to accelerate or delay its evolution according to the use which, consciously or unconsciously, we are continually making of it.

It would be hopeless within the limits of such a treatise as this to attempt to explain the different uses to which the forces inherent in the manifold varieties of this elemental essence can he put by one who has been trained in their management. The majority of magical ceremonies depend almost entirely upon its manipulation, either directly by the will of the magician, or by some more definite astral entity evoked by him for that purpose.

By its means nearly all the physical phenomena of the *séance*-room are produced, and it is also the agent in most cases of stone-throwing or bell-ringing in haunted houses, such results as these latter being brought about either by blundering efforts to attract attention made by some earth-bound human entity, or by the mere mischievous pranks of some of the minor nature-spirits belonging to our third class. But we must never think of the "elemental" as itself a prime mover; it is simply a latent force, which needs an external power to set it in motion.

Although all classes of the essence have the power of reflecting astral images as described above, there are varieties which receive certain impressions much more readily than others – which have, as it were, favourite forms of their own into which upon disturbance they would naturally flow unless absolutely forced into some other, and such shapes tend to be a trifle less evanescent than usual.

Before leaving this branch of the subject it may be well to warn the student against the confusion of thought into which some have fallen through failing to distinguish this elemental essence, which we have been considering from the monadic essence manifesting through the mineral kingdom.

Monadic essence at one stage of its evolution towards humanity manifests through the elemental kingdom, while at a later stage it manifests through the mineral kingdom; but the fact that two bodies of monadic essence at these different stages are in manifestation at the same moment, and that one of these manifestations (the earth elemental) occupies the same space as and inhabits the other (say a rock), in no way interferes with the evolution either of one or the other, nor does it imply any relation between the bodies of monadic essence lying within both.

2. *The Astral Bodies of Animals.* This is an extremely large class, yet it does not occupy a particularly important position on the astral plane, since its members usually stay there but a short time. The vast majority of animals have not as yet acquired permanent individualization, and when one of them dies the monadic essence which has been manifesting through it flows back again into the particular stratum whence it came, bearing with it such advancement or experience as has been attained during that life. It is not, however, able to do this quite immediately; the astral body of the animal rearranges itself just as in man's case, and the animal has a real existence on the astral plane, the length of which, though never great, varies according to the intelligence which it has developed. In most cases it does not seem to be more than dreamily conscious, but appears perfectly happy.

The comparatively few domestic animals who have already attained individuality, and will therefore be reborn no more as animals in this world, have a much longer and much more vivid life on the astral plane than their less advanced fellows, and at the end of it sink gradually into a subjective condition, which is likely to last for a very considerable period. One interesting subdivision of this class consists of the astral bodies of those anthropoid apes mentioned in *The Secret Doctrine,* who are already individualized, and will be ready to take human incarnation in the next round, or perhaps some of them even sooner.

3. *Nature-Spirits of all Kinds.* So many and so varied are the subdivisions of this class that to do them anything like justice one would need to devote a separate treatise to this subject alone. Some characteristics, however, they all have in common, and it will be sufficient here to try to give some idea of those.

First we have to realize that we are here dealing with entities which differ radically from all that we have hitherto considered. Though we may rightly classify the elemental essence and the animal astral bodies as non-human, the monadic essence which ensouls them will, nevertheless, in the fullness of time, evolve to the level of manifesting itself through some future humanity comparable to our own, and if we were able to look back through countless ages on our own evolution in previous world-cycles, we should find that that which is now our casual body has passed on its upward path through similar stages.

That, however, is not the case with the vast kingdom of nature-spirits; they neither have been, nor ever will be, members of a humanity such as ours; their line of evolution is entirely different, and their only connection with us consists in our temporary occupancy of the same planet. Of course since we are neighbours for the time being we owe neighbourly kindness to one another when we happen to meet, but our lines of development differ so widely that each can do but little for the other.

Many writers have included these spirits among the elementals, and indeed they are the elementals (or perhaps, to speak more accurately, the animals) of a higher evolution. Though much more highly developed than our elemental essence, they have yet certain characteristics in common with it; for example, they also are divided into seven great classes, inhabiting respectively the same seven states of matter already mentioned as permeated by the corresponding varieties of the essence. Thus, to take those, which are most readily comprehensible to us, there are spirits of the earth, water, air, and fire (or ether) – definite intelligent astral entities residing and functioning in each of those media.

It may be asked how it is possible for any kind of creature to inhabit the solid substance of a rock, or of the crust of the earth. The answer is that since the nature-spirits are formed of astral matter, the substance of the rock is no hindrance to their motion or their vision, and furthermore physical matter in its solid state is their natural element – that to which they are accustomed and in which they feel at home. The same is true of those who live in water, air, or ether.

In mediæval literature, these earth-spirits are often called gnomes, while the water-spirits are spoken of as undines, the air-spirits as sylphs, and the ether-spirits as salamanders. In popular language they are known by many names – fairies, pixies, elves, brownies, peris, djinns, trolls, satyrs, fauns, kobolds, imps, goblins, good people, etc. – some of these titles being applied only to one variety, and others indiscriminately to all.

Their forms are many and various, but most frequently human in shape and somewhat diminutive in size. Like almost all inhabitants of the astral plane, they are able to assume any appearance at will, but they undoubtedly have definite forms of their own, or perhaps we should rather say favourite forms, which they wear when they have no special object in taking an other. Under ordinary conditions they are

64

not visible to physical sight at all, but they have the power of making themselves so by materialization when they wish to be seen.

There are an immense number of subdivisions or races among them, and individuals differ in intelligence and disposition precisely as human beings do. The great majority of them apparently prefer to avoid man altogether; his habits and emanations are distasteful to them, and the constant rush of astral currents set up by his restless, ill-regulated desires disturbs and annoys them. On the other hand, instances are not wanting in which nature spirits have as it were made friends with human beings and offered them such assistance as lay in their power, as in the well-known stories told of the Scotch brownies or of the fire-lighting fairies mentioned in spiritualistic literature.

This helpful attitude, however, is comparatively rare, and in most cases when they come in contact with man they either show indifference or dislike, or else take an impish delight in deceiving him and playing childish tricks upon him. Many a story illustrative of this curious characteristic may be found among the village gossip of the peasantry in almost any lonely mountainous district; and any one who has been in the habit of attending *séances* for physical phenomena will recollect instances of practical joking and silly though usually good-natured horse-play, which almost always indicate the presence of some of the lower orders of the nature-spirits.

They are greatly assisted in their tricks by the wonderful power which they possess of casting a glamour over those who yield themselves to their influence, so that such victims for the time see and hear only what these fairies impress upon them, exactly as the mesmerized subject sees, hears, feels, and believes whatever the magnetizer wishes. The nature-spirits, however, have not the mesmerizer's power of dominating the human will, except in the case of quite unusually weak-minded people, or of those who allow themselves to fall into such a condition of helpless terror that their will is temporarily in abeyance. They cannot go beyond deception of the senses, but of that art they are undoubted masters, and cases are not wanting in which they have cast their glamour over a considerable number of people at once. It is by invoking their aid in the exercise of this peculiar power that some of the most wonderful feats of the Indian jugglers are performed – the entire audience being in fact hallucinated and made to imagine that they see and hear a whole series of events which have not really taken place at all.

We might almost look upon the nature-spirits as a kind of astral humanity, but for the fact that none of them – not even the highest – possesses a permanent reincarnating individuality. Apparently, therefore, one point in which their line of evolution differs from ours is that a much greater proportion of intelligence is developed before permanent individualization takes place; but of the stages through which they have passed, and those through which they have yet to pass, we can know little.

The life-periods of the different subdivisions vary greatly, some being quite short, others much longer than our human life-times. We stand so entirely outside such a life as theirs that it is impossible for us to understand much about its conditions; but it appears on the whole to be a simple, joyous, irresponsible kind of existence, such as a party of happy children might lead among exceptionally favourable physical surroundings.

Though tricky and mischievous, they are rarely malicious unless provoked by some unwarrantable intrusion or annoyance; but as a body they also partake to some extent of the universal feeling of distrust for man, and they generally seem inclined to resent somewhat the first appearance of a neophyte on the astral plane, so that he usually makes their acquaintance under some unpleasant or terrifying form. If, however, he declines to be frightened by any of their freaks, they soon accept him as a necessary evil and take no further notice of him, while some among them may even after a time become friendly and manifest pleasure on meeting him.

Some among the many subdivisions of this class are much less childlike and more dignified than those we have been describing, and it is from these sections that the lower types among the entities who have been reverenced under the name of wood-gods, or local village-gods, have been drawn. Such entities would be quite sensible of the flattery involved in the reverence shown to them, enjoy it, and are usually quite ready to do any small service they can in return. (The village-god is also often an artificial entity, but that variety will be considered in its appropriate place).

The Adept knows how to make use of the services of the nature-spirits when he requires them, but the ordinary magician can obtain their assistance only by processes either of invocation or evocation – that is, either by attracting their attention as a suppliant and making some kind of bargain with them, or by endeavouring to set in motion influences which would compel their obedience. Both methods are extremely undesirable, and the latter is also excessively dangerous, as the operator arouses a determined hostility which may easily prove fatal to him. Needless to say, no one studying occultism under a qualified Master would ever be permitted to attempt anything of the kind at all.

4. *The Devas.* The highest system of evolution connected with this earth, so far as we know, is that of the beings whom Hindus call the Devas, who are elsewhere described as Angels, sons of God, etc. They may, in fact, be regarded as a kingdom, lying next above humanity, in the same way as humanity in turn lies next above the animal kingdom, but with this important difference, that while for an animal there is no possibility of evolution (so far as we know) through any kingdom but the human man, when he attains a certain high level, finds various paths of advancement opening before him of which this great Deva evolution is only one.

In comparison with the sublime renunciation of the Nirmanakaya, the acceptance of this line of evolution is sometimes mentioned in the books as "yielding to the temptation to become a god", but it must not be inferred from this expression that any shadow of blame attaches to the man who makes this choice. The path which he selects is not the shortest, but it is nevertheless very noble, and if his developed intuition impels him towards it, it is certainly that which is best suited for his capacities. We must never forget that in spiritual as in physical climbing it is not every one who can bear the strain of the steeper path; there may be many for whom what seems the slower way is the only possiblity, and we should indeed be unworthy followers of the great Teachers if we allowed our ignorance to betray us into the slightest thought of disposal towards those whose choice differs from our own.

However confident ignorance of the difficulties of the future may allow us to feel now, it is impossible for us to tell at this stage what we shall find ourselves able to do when, after many lives of patient striving, we have earned the right to choose our own future; and indeed, even those who "yield to the temptation to become gods" have a sufficiently glorious career before them, as will presently be seen. To avoid possible misunderstanding it may be mentioned *par parenthése* that there is another and entirely evil sense sometimes attached in the books to this phrase of "becoming a god," but in that form it certainly could never be any kind of "temptation" to the developed man, and in any case it is altogether foreign to our present subject.

In oriental literature this word "Deva" is frequently used vaguely to mean almost any kind of non-human entity, so that it often includes great divinities on the one hand, and nature-spirits and artificial elementals on the other. Here, however, its use will be restricted to the magnificent evolution which we are now considering.

Though connected with this earth, the Angels are by no means confined to it, for the whole of our present chain of seven worlds is as one world to them, their evolution being through a grand system of seven chains. Their hosts have hitherto been recruited chiefly from other humanities in the solar system, some lower and some higher than ours, since but a very small portion of our own has as yet reached the level at which for us it is possible to join them; but it seems certain that some of their very numerous classes have not passed in their upward progress through any humanity at all comparable to ours.

It is not possible for us at present to understand much about them, but it is clear that what may be described as the aim of their evolution is considerably higher than ours; that is to say, while the object of our human evolution is to raise the successful portion of humanity to a certain degree of occult development by the end of the seventh round, the object of the angelic evolution is to bring their foremost rank to a much higher level in the corresponding period. For them, as for us, a steeper but shorter path to still more sublime heights lies open to earnest endeavour; but what those heights may be in their case we can only conjecture.

It is only the lower fringe of this august body that need be mentioned in connection with our subject of the astral plane. Their three lower great divisions (beginning from the bottom) are generally called Kamadevas, Rupadevas, and Arupadevas respectively. Just as our ordinary body here – the lowest body possible for us – is the physical, so the ordinary body of a Kamadeva is the astral; so that he stands in somewhat the same position as humanity will do when it reaches planet F, and he, living ordinarily in an astral body, goes out of it to higher spheres in a mental vehicle just as we do in an astral body, while to enter the causal body is to him (when sufficiently developed) no greater effort than to use a mind body is to us.

In the same way the Rupadeva's ordinary body is the mental, since his habitat is on the four lower or rupa levels of that plane; while the Arupadeva belongs to the three higher levels, and owns no nearer approach to a body than the causal. But for Rupa and Arupa devas to manifest on the astral plane is an occurrence at least as rare as it is for astral entities to materialize on this physical plane, so we need do no more than mention them now.

As regards the lowest division – the Kamadevas – it would be a mistake to think of all of them as immeasurably superior to ourselves, since some have entered their ranks from humanity in some respects less advanced than our own. The general average among them is much higher than among us, for all that is actively or willfully evil has long been weeded out from their ranks; but they differ widely in disposition, and a really noble, unselfish, spiritually-minded man may well stand higher in the scale of evolution than some of them.

Their attention can be attracted by certain magical evocations, but the only human will which can dominate theirs is that of a certain high class of Adepts. As a rule they seem scarcely conscious of *us* on our physical plane, but it does now and then happen that one of them becomes aware of some human difficulty which excites his pity, and he perhaps renders some assistance, just as any of us would try to help an animal that we saw in trouble. But it is well understood among them that any interference in human affairs at the present stage is likely to do far more harm than good. Above the Arupadevas there are four other great divisions, and again, above and beyond the angelic kingdom altogether, stand the great hosts of the Planetary Spirits, but the consideration of such glorified beings would be out of place in an essay on the astral plane.

Though we cannot claim them as belonging exactly to any of our classes, this is perhaps the best place in which to mention those wonderful and important beings, the four Devarajas. In this name the word Deva must not, however, be taken in the sense in which we have been using it, for it is not over the Deva kingdom, but over the four, "elements" of earth, water, air, and fire, with their indwelling naturespirits and essences, that these four Kings rule. What the evolution has been through which they rose to their present height of power and wisdom we cannot tell, save only that it does not seem to have passed through anything corresponding to our own humanity.

They are often described as the Regents of the Earth, or Angels of the four cardinal points, and the Hindu books call them the Chatur Maharajas, giving their names as Dhritarashtra, Virudhaka, Virupaksha, and Vaishravana. In the same books their elemental hosts are called Gandharvas, Kumbhandas, Nagas, and Yakshas respectively, the points of the compass appropriated to each being in corresponding order east, south, west, and north, and their symbolical colours, white, blue, red, and gold. They are mentioned in

70

The Secret Doctrine as "winged globes and fiery wheels"; and in the Christian bible Ezekiel makes a remarkable attempt at a description of them in which similar words are used. References to them are to be found in the symbology of every religion, and they have always been held in the highest reverence as the protectors of mankind.

It is they who are the agents of man's karma during his life on earth, and they thus play an extremely important part in human destiny. The great karmic deities of the Kosmos (called in *The Secret Doctrine* the Lipika) weigh the deeds of each personality when the final separation of its principles takes place at the end of its astral life, and give as it were the mould of an etheric double exactly suitable to its karma for the man s next birth; but it is the Devarajas who, having command of the "elements" of which that etheric double must be composed, arrange their proportion so as to fulfil accurately the intention of the Lipika.

It is they also who constantly watch all through life to counterbalance the changes perpetually being introduced into man's condition by his own free will and that of those around him, so that no injustice may be done, and karma may be accurately worked out, if not in one way then in another. They are able to take human material forms at will, and several cases are recorded when they have done so.

All the higher nature-spirits and hosts of artificial elementals act as their agents in the stupendous work they carry out, yet all the threads are in their hands, and the whole responsibility rests upon them alone. It is not often that they manifest upon the astral plane, but when they do they are certainly the most remarkable of its non-human inhabitants. A student of occultism will not need to be told that as there are seven great classes both of nature-spirits and elemental essence there must really be seven and not four Devarajas, but outside the circle of Initiation little is known and less may be said of the higher three.

III. ARTIFICIAL

This, the largest class of astral entities, is also much the most important to man. Being entirely his own creation, it is inter-related with him by the closest karmic bonds, and its action upon him is direct and incessant. It is an enormous inchoate mass of semi-intelligent entities, differing among themselves as human thoughts differ, and practically incapable of anything like classification or arrangement. The only division which can be usefully made is that which distinguishes between the artificial elementals made by the majority of mankind unconsciously, and those made by magicians with definite intent; while we may relegate to a third class the small number of artificially arranged entities which are not elementals at all.

1. *Elementals formed unconsciously.* I have explained that the elemental essence which surrounds us on every side is in all its numberless varieties singularly susceptible to the influence of human thought. The action of the mere casual wandering thought upon it, causing it to burst into a cloud of rapidly-moving, evanescent forms, has been described; we have now to note how it is affected when the human mind formulates a definite, purposeful thought or wish.

The effect produced is of the most striking nature. The thought seizes upon the plastic essence, and moulds it instantly into a living being of appropriate form – a being which when once thus created is in no way under the control of its creator, but lives out a life of its own, the length of which is proportionate to the intensity of the thought or wish which called it into existence. It lasts, in fact, just as long as the thought-force holds it together. Most people's thoughts are so fleeting and indecisive that the elementals created by them last only a few minutes or a few hours, but an often-repeated thought or an earnest wish will form an elemental whose existence may extend to many days.

Since the ordinary man's thoughts refer largely to himself, the elementals which they form remain hovering about him, and constantly tend to provoke a repetition of the idea which they represent, since such repetitions, instead of forming new elementals, strengthen that already in existence, and give it a fresh lease of life. A man, therefore, who frequently dwells upon one wish often forms for himself an astral attendant which, constantly fed by fresh thought, may haunt him for years, ever gaining more and more strength and influence over him; and it will easily be seen that if the desire be evil the effect upon his moral nature may be of a disastrous character.

Still more pregnant of result for good or evil are a man's thoughts about other people, for, in that case they hover not about the thinker, but about the object of the thought. A kindly thought about any person, or an earnest wish for his good, forms and projects towards him a friendly, artificial elemental. If the wish be definite, as, for example, that he may recover from some sickness, then the elemental will be a force ever hovering over him to promote his recovery, or to ward off any influence that might tend to hinder it. In doing this it will display, what appears like a very considerable amount of intelligence and adaptability, though really it is a force acting along the line of least resistance – pressing steadily in one direction all the time, and taking advantage of any channel that it can find, as the water in a cistern would in a moment find the one open pipe among a dozen closed, and proceed to empty itself through that.

If the wish be merely indefinite, for his general good, the elemental essence in its wonderful plasticity will respond exactly to that less distinct idea also, and the creature formed will expend its force in the direction of whatever action for the man's advantage comes most readily to hand. In all cases the amount of such force which it has to expend, and the length of time that it will live to expend it, depend entirely upon the strength of the original wish or thought which gave it birth; though it must be remembered that it can be, as it were, fed and strengthened, and its life-period protracted by other good wishes or friendly thoughts projected in the same direction.

Furthermore, it appears to be actuated, like most other beings, by an instinctive desire to prolong its life, and thus reacts on its creator as a force constantly tending to provoke the renewal of the feeling which called it into existence. It also influences in a similar manner others with whom it comes into contact, though its *rapport* with them is naturally not so perfect.

All that has been said as to the effect of good wishes and friendly thoughts is also true in the opposite direction of evil wishes and angry thoughts; and considering the amount of envy, hatred, malice, and all uncharitableness that exists in the world, it will be readily understood that among the artificial elementals many terrible creatures are to be seen. A man whose thoughts or desires are spiteful, brutal, sensual, avaricious, moves through the world carrying with him everywhere a pestiferous atmosphere of his own, peopled with the loathsome beings which he has created to be his companions. Thus he is not only in sadly evil case himself, but is a dangerous nuisance to his fellowmen, subjecting all who have the misfortune to come into contact with him to the risk of moral contagion from the influence of the abominations with which he chooses to surround himself.

A feeling of envious or jealous hatred towards another person sends an evil elemental to hover over him and seek for a weak point through which it can operate; and if the feeling be persistent, such a creature may be continually nourished by it and thereby enabled to protract its undesirable activity for a long period. It can, however, produce no effect upon the person towards whom it is directed unless he has himself some tendency which it can foster – some fulcrum for its lever, as it were. From the aura of a man of pure thought and good life all such influences at once rebound, finding nothing upon which they can fasten, and in that case, by a curious law, they react in all their force upon their original creator. In him by the hypothesis they find a congenial sphere of action, and thus the karma of his evil wish works itself out at once by means of the very entity which he himself has called into existence.

It occasionally happens, however, that an artificial elemental of this description is for various reasons unable to expend its force either upon its object or its creator, and in such cases it becomes a kind of wandering demon. It is readily attracted by any person who indulges in feelings similar to that which gave it birth, and equally prepared either to stimulate such feelings in him for the sake of the strength it may gain from them, or to pour out its store of evil influence upon him through any opening which he may offer it. If it is sufficiently powerful to seize upon and inhabit some passing shell it frequently does so, as the possession of such a temporary home enables it to husband its dreadful resources more carefully. In this form it may manifest through a medium, and by masquerading as some well-known friend may sometimes obtain an influence over people upon whom it would otherwise have little hold.

What is written above will serve to enforce the statement already made as to the importance of maintaining a strict control over our thoughts. Many a well-meaning man, who is scrupulously careful to do his duty towards his neighbour in word and deed, is apt to consider that his thoughts at least are nobody's business but his own, and so lets them run riot in various directions, utterly unconscious of the swarms of baleful creatures which he is launching upon the world.

To such a man an accurate comprehension of the effect of thought and desire in producing artificial elementals would come as a horrifying revelation; on the other hand, it would be the greatest consolation to many devoted and grateful souls who are oppressed with the feeling that they are unable to do anything in return for the kindness lavished upon them by their benefactors. For friendly thoughts and earnest good wishes are as easily and as effectually formulated by the poorest as by the richest, and it is within the power of almost any man, if he will take the trouble, to maintain what is practically a good angel always at the side of the brother or sister, the friend or the child, whom he loves best, no matter in what part of the world he may be.

Many a time a mother's loving thoughts and prayers have formed themselves into an angel guardian for the child, and except in the almost impossible case that the child had in him no instinct responsive to a good influence, have undoubtedly given him assistance and protection. Such guardians may often be seen by clairvoyant vision, and there have even been cases in which one of them has had sufficient strength to materialize and become for the moment visible to physical sight.

A curious fact which deserves mention here is that even after the passage of the mother into the heaven-world the love which she pours out upon the children whom she imagines as surrounding her, will react upon those children though they are still living in this world, and will often support the guardian elemental which she created while on earth, until those children themselves pass away in turn. As Madame Blavatsky remarks, "her love will always be felt by the children in the flesh; it will manifest in their dreams and often in various events, in providential protections and escapes – for love is a strong shield, and is not limited by space or time". All the stories of the intervention of guardian Angels must not, however, be attributed to the action of artificial elementals, for in many cases such "angels" have been either living or recently departed human beings, and they have also occasionally, though rarely, been Devas.

This power of an earnest desire, especially if frequently repeated, to create an active elemental which ever passes forcefully in the direction of its own fulfillment, is the scientific explanation of what devout but unphilosophical people describe as answers to prayer. There are occasions, though at present these are rare, when the karma of the person so praying is such as to permit of assistance being directly rendered to him by an Adept or his pupil, and there is also the still rarer possibility of the intervention of a Deva or some friendly nature-spirit; but in all these cases the easiest and most obvious form for such assistance to take would be the strengthening and the intelligent direction of the elemental already formed by the wish.

A curious and instructive instance of the extreme persistence of these artificial elementals under favourable circumstances came some time ago under the notice of one of our investigators. All readers of the literature of such subjects are aware that many of our ancient families are supposed to have associated with them a traditional death-warning – a phenomenon of one kind or another which foretells, usually some days beforehand, the approaching decease of the head of the house. A picturesque example of this is the well-known story of the white bird of the Oxenhams, whose appearance has ever since the time of Queen Elizabeth been recognised as a sure presage of the death of some member of the family; while another is the spectral coach which is reported to drive up to the door of a certain castle in the north when a similar calamity is impending.

A phenomenon of this order occurs in connection with the family of one of our members, but it is of a much commoner and less striking type than either of the above, consisting only of a solemn and impressive strain of dirgelike music, which is heard apparently floating in the air three days before the death takes place. Our member, having himself twice heard this mystic sound, finding its warning in both cases quite accurate, and knowing also that according to family tradition the same thing had been happening for several centuries, set himself to seek by occult methods for the cause underlying so strange a phenomenon.

The result was unexpected but interesting. It appeared that somewhere in the twelfth century the head of the family went to the crusades, like many another valiant man, and took with him to win his spurs in the sacred cause his youngest and favourite son, a promising youth whose success in life was the dearest wish of his father's heart. Unhappily, however, the young man was killed in battle, and the father was plunged into the depths of despair, lamenting not only the loss of his son, but still more the fact that he was cut off so suddenly in the full flush of careless and not altogether blameless youth.

So poignant, indeed, were the old man's feelings that he cast off his knightly armour and joined one of the great monastic orders, vowing to devote all the remainder of his life to prayer, first for the soul of his son, and secondly that henceforward no descendant of his might ever again encounter what seemed to his simple and pious mind the terrible danger of meeting death unprepared. Day after day for many a year he poured all the energy of his soul into the channel of that one intense wish, firmly believing that somehow or other the result he so earnestly desired would be brought about.

A student of occultism will have little difficulty in deciding what would be the effect of such a definite and long-continued stream of thought; our knightly monk created an artificial elemental of immense power and resourcefulness for its own particular object, and accumulated within it a store of force which would enable it to carry out his wishes for an indefinite period. An elemental is a perfect storage-battery, from which there is practically no leakage; and when we remember what its original strength must have been, and how comparatively rarely it would be called upon to put it forth, we shall scarcely wonder that even now it exhibits unimpaired vitality, and still warns the direct descendants of the old crusader of their approaching doom by repeating in their ears the strange walling music which was the dirge of a young and valiant soldier eight hundred years ago in Palestine.

2. *Elementals formed consciously.* Since such results as have been described above have been achieved by the thought-force of men who were entirely in the dark as to what they were doing, it will readily be imagined that a magician who understands the subject, and can see exactly what effect he is producing, may wield immense power along these lines. As a matter of fact occultists of both the white and dark schools frequently use artificial elementals in their work, and few tasks are beyond the powers of such creatures when scientifically prepared and directed with knowledge and skill; for one who knows how to do so can maintain a connection with his elemental and guide it, no matter at what distance it may be working, so that it will practically act as though endowed with the full intelligence of its master.

Definite and efficient guardian Angels have sometimes been supplied in this way, though it is probably rarely that karma permits such a decided interference in a person's life as that would be. In such a case, however, as that of a pupil of the Adepts, who might have in the course of his work for Them to run the risk of attack from forces with which his unaided strength would be entirely insufficient to cope, guardians of this description have been given, and have fully proved their sleepless vigilance and their tremendous power.

By some of the more advanced processes of black magic, also, artificial elementals of great power may be called into existence, and much evil has been worked in various ways by such entities. But it is true of them, as of the previous class, that if they are aimed at a person whom by reason of his purity of character they are unable to influence, they react with terrible force upon their creator; so that the mediæval story of the magician being torn to pieces by the fiends he himself had raised is no mere fable, but may well have a definite foundation in fact.

Such creatures occasionally, for various reasons, escape from the control of those who are trying to make use of them, and become wandering and aimless demons, as do some of those mentioned under the previous heading in similar circumstances; but those that we are considering, having much more intelligence and power, and a much longer existence, are proportionately more dangerous. They invariably seek for means of prolonging their lives, either by feeding, like vampires, upon the vitality of human beings, or by influencing them to make offerings to them; and among simple half-savage tribes they have frequently succeeded by judicious management in being recognized as village or family gods.

Any deity which demands sacrifices involving the shedding of blood may always be set down as belonging to the lowest and most loathsome class of this order; other less objectionable types are sometimes content with offerings of rice and cooked food of various kinds. There are parts of India where both these varieties may be found flourishing even at the present day, and in Africa they are probably comparatively numerous.

By means of whatever nourishment they can obtain from the offerings, and still more by the vitality they draw from their devotees, they may continue to prolong their existence for many years, or even centuries, retaining sufficient strength to perform occasional phenomena of a mild type in order to stimulate the faith and zeal of their followers, and invariably making themselves unpleasant in some way or other if the accustomed sacrifices are neglected. For example, it is asserted that in one Indian village the inhabitants have found that whenever for any reason the local deity is not provided with his or her regular meals, spontaneous fires began to break out with alarming frequency among the cottages, sometimes three or four simultaneously, in cases where they declare it is impossible to suspect human agency; and other stories of a more or less similar nature will no doubt recur to the memory of any reader who knows something of the out-of-the-way corners of that most wonderful of all countries.

The art of manufacturing artificial elementals of extreme virulence and power seems to have been one of the specialties of the magicians of Atlantis – "the lords of the dark face." One example of their capabilities in this line is given in *The Secret Doctrine*, where we read of the wonderful speaking animals who had to be quieted by an offering of blood, lest they should awaken their masters and warn them of the impending destruction. But apart from these strange beasts they created other artificial entities of power and energy so tremendous, that it is darkly hinted that some of them have kept themselves in existence even to this day, though it is more than eleven thousand years since the cataclysm which overwhelmed their original masters. The terrible Indian goddess whose devotees were impelled to commit in her name the awful crimes of Thuggee – the ghastly Kali, worshipped even to this day with rites too abominable to be described – might well be a relic of a system which had to be swept away even at the cost of the submergence of a continent, and the loss of sixty-five million human lives.

3. *Human Artificials.* We have now to consider a class of entities which, though it contains but few individuals, has acquired from its intimate connection with one of the great movements of modern times an importance entirely out of proportion to its numbers. It seems doubtful whether it should appear under the first or third of our main divisions;

but, though certainly human, it is so far removed from the course of ordinary evolution, so entirely the product of a will outside of its own, that it perhaps falls most naturally into place among the artificial beings.

The easiest way of describing it will be to commence with its history, and to do that we must once more look back to the great Atlantean race. In thinking of the Adepts and schools of occultism of that remarkable people our minds instinctively revert to the evil practices of which we hear so much in connection with their latter days; but we must not forget that before that age of selfishness and degradation, the mighty civilization of Atlantis had brought forth much that was noble and worthy of admiration, and that among its leaders were some who now stand upon the loftiest pinnacles as yet attained by man.

Among the lodges for occult study preliminary to Initiation formed by the Adepts of the good Law was one in a certain part of America which was then tributary to one of the great Atlantean monarchs – "the Divine Rulers of the Golden Gate"; and though it has passed through many and strange vicissitudes, though it has had to move its headquarters from country to country as each in turn was invaded by the jarring elements of a later civilization, that Lodge still exists even at the present day, observing still the same old-world ritual – even teaching as a sacred and hidden language the same Atlantean tongue which was used at its foundation so many thousands of years ago.

It still remains what it was from the first – a Lodge of occultists of pure and philanthropic aims, which can lead those students whom it finds worthy no inconsiderable distance on the road to knowledge, and confers such psychic powers as are in its gift only after the most searching tests as to the fitness of the candidate. Its teachers do not stand upon the Adept level, yet hundreds have learnt through it how to set their feet upon the Path which has led them to Adeptship in later lives; and though it is not directly a part of the Brotherhood of the Himalayas, there are some among the latter who have Themselves been connected with it in former incarnations, and therefore retain a more than ordinarily friendly interest in its proceedings. Indeed. I well remember how the present Leader of that Lodge, on seeing the portrait of one of the Masters of Wisdom, at once prostrated himself before it in deepest reverence.

The Chiefs of this Lodge, though they have always kept themselves and their society strictly in the background, have nevertheless done what they could from time to time to assist the progress of truth in the world. Nearly a century ago, in despair at the rampant materialism which seemed to be stifling all spirituality in Europe and America, they determined to make an attempt to combat it by somewhat novel methods – in point of fact to offer opportunities by which any reasonable man could acquire absolute proof of that life apart from the physical body which it was the tendency of science to deny. The phenomena exhibited were not in themselves absolutely new, since in some form or other we may hear of them all through history; but their definite organization – their production as it were to order – these were features distinctly new to the modern world.

The movement which they thus set on foot gradually grew into the vast fabric of modern Spiritualism, and though it would perhaps be unfair to hold the originators of the scheme directly responsible for many of the results which have followed, we must admit that they have achieved their purpose to the extent of converting vast numbers of people from a belief in nothing in particular to a firm faith in at any rate some kind of future life. This is undoubtedly a magnificent result, though there are those who think that it has been attained at too great a cost.

The method adopted was to take some ordinary person after death, arouse him thoroughly upon the astral plane, instruct him to a certain extent in the powers and possibilities belonging to it, and then put him in charge of a Spiritualistic circle. He in his turn "developed" other departed personalities along the same line, they all acted upon those who sat at their *séances,* and "developed" them as mediums; and so spiritualism grew and flourished. No doubt living members of the original Lodge occasionally manifested themselves in astral form at some of the circles – perhaps they may do so even now; but in most cases they contented themselves with giving such direction and guidance as they considered necessary to the persons they had put in charge. There is little doubt that the movement increased so much more rapidly than they had expected that it soon got quite beyond their control, so that, as has been said, for many of the later developments they can only be held indirectly responsible.

The intensification of the astral-plane life in those persons who were thus put in charge of circles some-what delayed their natural progress; and though the idea had been that anything lost in this way would be fully compensated by the good karma gained by helping to lead others to the truth, it was soon found that it was impossible to make use of a "spirit-guide" for any length of time without doing him serious and permanent injury. In some cases such "guides" were therefore withdrawn, and others substituted for them; in others it was considered for various reasons undesirable make such a change, and then a remarkable expedient was adopted which gave rise to the curious class of creatures we have called "human artificials."

The higher principles of the original "guide" were allowed to pass on their long-delayed evolution into the heaven-world, but the shade which he left behind him was occupied, sustained, and strengthened so that it might appear to its admiring circle practically just as before. This seems at first to have been done by members of the Lodge themselves, but apparently that arrangement was found irksome or unsuitable, or perhaps was considered a waste of force, and the same objection applied to the use for this purpose of an artificial elemental; so it was eventually decided that the departed person who would have been appointed to succeed the late "spirit-guide" should still do so, but should take possession of the latter's shade or shell, and in fact simply wear his appearance.

It is said that some members of the Lodge objected to this on the ground that though the purpose might be entirely good, a certain amount of deception was involved; but the general opinion seems to have been that as the shade really was the same, and contained something at any rate of the original lower mind, there was nothing that could be called deception in the matter. This, then, was the genesis of the human artificial entity, and it is understood that in some cases more than one such change has been made without arousing suspicion, though on the other hand some investigators of spiritualism have remarked on the fact that after a considerable lapse of time certain differences suddenly became observable in the manner and disposition of a "spirit." It is needless to say that none of the Adept Brotherhood has ever undertaken the formation of an artificial entity of this sort, though They could not interfere with any one who thought it right to take such a course. A weak point in the arrangement is that many others besides the original Lodge may adopt this plan, and there is nothing whatever to prevent black magicians from supplying communicating "spirits" – as, indeed, they have been known to do.

With this class we conclude our survey of the inhabitants of the astral plane. With the reservations specially made some few pages back, the catalogue may be taken as fairly complete; but it must once more be emphasized that this treatise claims only to sketch the merest outline of a very vast subject, the detailed elaboration of which would need a lifetime of study and hard work.

CHAPTER IV
PHENOMENA

FROM one point of view this should have been the first chapter of our book instead of the last, for it was from the consideration of its subject-matter that all the rest arose. I owe my introduction to Theosophy in this incarnation to our then Vice-President, Mr. A. P. Sinnett, who was always exceptionally kind to me, and while I was staying with him we used to meet every Sunday morning in his library to discuss Theosophical matters. On one such occasion he casually remarked that he did not think that the Theosophical teaching so far given to us adequately covered or accounted for many of the spiritualistic phenomena which both of us had repeatedly seen. Rather startled by this hypothesis I stoutly maintained the opinion that they were satisfactorily covered, and proceeded to give examples.

Mr. Sinnett seemed favourably impressed, and asked me to give a lecture to the London Lodge expounding my views. I agreed to do this, but when I came to prepare that lecture I soon found that in order to make myself intelligible I must begin by a general description of the astral world as a whole, with its conditions and the powers and possibilities of its inhabitants. I realized that I had undertaken a larger contract than I intended; but clearly it was a piece of work that had to be done, so I might as well go ahead and do it to the best of my ability.

Though in the course of this manual various super-physical phenomena have been mentioned and to some extent explained, it will perhaps before concluding be desirable so far to recapitulate as to give a list of those with which the student of these subjects most frequently meets, and to show by which of the agencies we have attempted to describe they are usually caused. The resources of the astral world, however, are so varied that almost any phenomenon with which we are acquainted can be produced in several different ways, so that it is only possible to lay down general rules in the matter.

Apparitions or ghosts furnish a very good instance of the remark just made, for in the loose manner in which the words are ordinarily used they may stand for almost any inhabitant of the astral plane. Psychically developed people are constantly seeing such things, but for an ordinary person to "see a ghost", as the common expression runs, one of two things must happen: either that ghost must materialize, or that person must have a temporary flash of psychic perception. But for the fact that neither of these events is common, we should meet with ghosts in our streets as frequently as living people.

CHURCHYARD GHOSTS
If the ghost is seen hovering about a grave it is probably the etheric shell of a newly buried person, though it *may* be the

astral body of a living man haunting in sleep the tomb of a friend; or again, it may be a materialized thought form – that is, an artificial elemental created by the energy with which a man thinks of himself as present at that particular spot. These varieties would be easily distinguishable one from the other by any one accustomed to use astral vision, but an unpractised person would be likely to call them all vaguely "ghosts".

APPARITIONS OF THE DYING
Apparitions at the time of death are by no means uncommon, and are often really visits paid by the astral form of the dying man just before what we elect to call the moment of dissolution; though here again they are just as likely to be thought-forms called into being by his earnest wish to see some friend once more before he passes into an unfamiliar condition. There are some instances in which the visit is paid just after the moment of death instead of just before; and in such a case the visitor is really a ghost; but for various causes this form of apparition is far less frequent than the other.

HAUNTED LOCALITIES
Apparitions at the spot where some crime was committed are usually thought-forms projected by the criminal; for the ordinary criminal, whether living or dead, but most especially when dead, is perpetually thinking over again and again the circumstances of his action. Since these thoughts are naturally specially vivid in his mind on the anniversary of the original crime, it is often only on that occasion that the thought-forms which he creates are strong enough to materialize themselves to ordinary sight – a fact which accounts for the periodicity of some manifestations of this class. Habitual criminals are frequently too callous to be especially moved by the recollection of one particular crime, but in that case other factors might come into play.

Another point in reference to such phenomena is that, wherever any tremendous mental disturbance has taken place, wherever overwhelming terror, pain, sorrow, hatred, or indeed any kind of intense passion has been felt, an impression of so marked a character has been made upon the astral matter that a person with even the faintest glimmer of psychic faculty cannot but be deeply impressed by it. It would need but a slight temporary increase of sensibility to enable him to visualize the entire scene – to see the event in all its detail apparently taking place before his eyes – and in such a case he would report that the place was haunted, and that he had seen a ghost.

People who are yet unable to see psychically under any circumstances are frequently unpleasantly impressed when visiting such places as we have mentioned. There are many, for example, who feel uncomfortable when passing the site of Tyburn Tree, or cannot stay in the Chamber of Horrors at Madame Tussaud's, though they may not be in the least aware that their discomfort is due to the dreadful impressions in the astral matter which surround places and objects redolent of horror and crime, and to the presence of the loathsome astral entities which always swarm about such centres.

FAMILY GHOSTS

The family ghost, whom we generally find in the stock stories of the supernatural as an appanage of the feudal castle, may be either a thought-form or an unusually vivid impression in astral matter, or again he may really be an earth-bound ancestor still haunting the scenes in which his thoughts and hopes centred during life.

BELL-RINGING, STONE-THROWING, ETC.

Another class of hauntings, which take the form of bell-ringing, stonethrowing, or the breaking of crockery, has already been mentioned, and is almost invariably the work of elemental forces, either set blindly in motion by the clumsy efforts of an ignorant person trying to attract the attention of is surviving friends, or intentionally employed by some childishly mischievous nature-spirit. To such manifestations the name *poltergeist* is usually given.

FAIRIES

The nature-spirits are also responsible for whatever of truth may be in all the fairy stories, which are so common in certain country places. Sometimes a temporary accession of clairvoyance, which is by no means uncommon among the inhabitants of lonely mountainous regions, enables some belated wayfarer to watch their joyous gambols; sometimes strange tricks are played upon some terrified victim, and a glamour is cast over him, making him, for example, see houses and people where he knows none really exist. And this is frequently no mere momentary delusion, for a man will sometimes go through quite a long series of imaginary but most striking adventures, and then suddenly find that all his brilliant surroundings have vanished in a moment, leaving him standing in some lonely valley or on some wind-swept plain. On the other hand, it is by no means safe to accept as founded on fact all the popular legends on the subject, for the grossest superstition is often mingled with the theories of the peasantry about these beings, as has been shown sometimes by terrible murder cases.

To the same entities must he attributed a large portion of what are called physical phenomena at spiritualistic *séances* – indeed, many a *séance* has been given entirely by these mischievous creatures. Such a performance might easily include many very striking items, such as the answering of questions and delivery of pretended messages by raps or tilts, the exhibition of "spirit lights," the apport of objects from a distance, the reading of thoughts which were in the mind of any person present, the precipitation of writings or drawings, and even materializations.

In fact, the nature-spirits alone, if any of them happened to he disposed to take the trouble, could give a *séance* equal to the most wonderful of which we read; for though there may be certain phenomena which they would not find it easy to reproduce, their marvellous power of glamour would enable them without difficulty to persuade the entire circle that these phenomena also had duly occurred – unless, indeed, there were present a trained observer who understood their arts and knew how to defeat them. As a general rule, whenever silly tricks or practical jokes are played at a *séance*, we may infer the presence either of lowclass nature-spirits, or of human beings who were of a sufficiently degraded type to find pleasure in such idiotic performances during life.

COMMUNICATING ENTITIES

As to the entities who may "communicate" at a *séance* or may obsess and speak through an entranced medium, their name is simply legion; there is hardly a single class among all the varied inhabitants of the astral plane from whose ranks they may not be drawn, though after the explanations given it will be readily understood that the chances are against their coming from an exalted level. A manifesting "spirit" is often exactly what it professes to be, especially at a private *séance* conducted by educated and serious people; but often also it is nothing of the kind; and for the ordinary sitter there is no means of distinguishing the true from the false, since the extent to which a being having all the resources of the astral plane at his command can delude a person on the physical plane is so great that no reliance can be placed even on what seems at first sight to be the most convincing proof.

If something manifests which announces itself as a man's long-lost brother, he can have no certainty that its claim is just. If it tells him of some fact known only to that brother and to himself, he remains unconvinced, for he knows that it might easily have read the information from his own mind, or from his surroundings in the astral world. Even if it goes still further and tells him something connected with his brother, of which he himself is unaware, but which he afterwards verifies, he still realizes that even this may have been read from the astral record, or that what he sees before him may be only the shade of his brother, and so possess his memory without in any way being himself. It is not for one moment denied that important communications have been made at *séances* by entities who in such cases have been precisely what they said they were; all that is claimed is that it is quite impossible for the ordinary person who visits a *séance* (especially a public *séance*) ever to be certain that he is not being cruelly deceived in one or other of half a dozen different ways.

There have been a few cases in which members of the Lodge of occultists referred to above as originating the spiritualistic movement have themselves given, through a medium, a series of valuable teachings on deeply interesting subjects, but this has invariably been at strictly private family *séances,* not at public performances for which money has been paid.

ASTRAL RESOURCES

To understand the methods by which a large class of physical phenomena are produced, it is necessary to have some comprehension of the various resources mentioned above, which a person functioning on the astral plane finds at his command; and this is a branch of the subject which it is by no means easy to make clear, especially as it is hedged about with certain obviously necessary restrictions. It may perhaps help us if we remember that the astral world may be regarded as in many ways only an extension of the physical, and the idea that matter may assume the etheric state (in which, though intangible to us, it is yet purely physical) may serve to show us how the one melts into the other. In fact, in the Hindu conception of Jagrat, or "the waking state," the physical and astral planes are combined, its seven subdivisions corresponding to the four conditions of physical matter, and the three broad divisions of astral matter, which have previously been explained.

With this thought in our minds it is easy to move a step further, and grasp the idea that astral vision, or rather astral perception, may from one point of view be defined as the capability of receiving an enormously increased number of different sets of vibrations. In our physical bodies one small set of vibrations is perceptible to us as sound; another small set of much more rapid vibrations affects us as light; and again another set as electric action; but there are immense numbers of intermediate vibrations which produce no result which our physical senses can cognize at all. It will readily be seen that if all, or even some only, of these intermediates, with all the complications producible by differences of wave-length, are perceptible on the astral plane, our comprehension of nature might be greatly increased on that level, and we might be able to acquire much information which is now hidden from us.

CLAIRVOYANCE

It is admitted that some of these vibrations pass through solid matter with perfect ease, so that this enables us to account scientifically for the peculiarities of etheric vision, though for astral sight the theory of the fourth dimension gives a neater and more complete explanation. It is clear that the mere possession of this astral vision by a being would at once account for his capability to produce many results that seem wonderful to us – such, for example, as the reading of a passage from a closed book. When we remember, furthermore, that this faculty includes the power of thought-reading (in so far as that thought affects emotions), and also, when combined with the knowledge of the projection of currents in the astral currents, that of observing a desired object in almost any part of the world, we see that many of the phenomena of clairvoyance are explicable even without rising above this level. I would refer any one who desires to study more closely this interesting subject to my little book, *Clairvoyance*, in which its varieties are tabulated and explained, and numerous examples given.

PREVISION AND SECOND-SIGHT

True, trained, and absolutely reliable clairvoyance calls into operation an entirely different set of faculties, but as these belong to a higher plane than the astral, they form no part of our present subject. The faculty of accurate prevision, again, appertains altogether to that higher plane, yet flashes or reflections of it frequently show themselves to purely astral sight, more especially among simple-minded people who live under suitable conditions – what is called "secondsight" among the Highlanders of Scotland being a wellknown example.

Another fact which we must not forget is that any intelligent inhabitant of the astral plane is not only able to perceive these etheric vibrations, but can also – if he has learnt how it is done – adapt them to his own ends, or himself set them in motion.

ASTRAL FORCES

Super-physical forces and the methods of managing them are not subjects about which much can be written for publication at present, though there is reason to suppose that it may not be long before at any rate some application of one or two of them come to be known to the world at large; but it may perhaps be possible, without transgressing the limits of the permissible, to give so much of an idea of them as shall be sufficient to show in outline how certain phenomena are performed.

All who have much experience of spiritualistic *séances* at which physical results are produced must at one time or another have seen evidence of the employment of practically resistless force in, for example, the instantaneous movement of enormous weights, and so on; and if of a scientific turn of mind, they may perhaps have wondered whence this force was obtained, and what was the leverage employed. As usual in connection with astral phenomena, there are several ways in which such work may have been done, but it will be enough for the moment to hint at four.

ETHERIC CURRENTS
First, there are great etheric currents constantly sweeping over the surface of the earth from pole to pole in volume which makes their power as irresistible as that of the rising tide, and there are methods by which this stupendous force may be safely utilized, though unskillful attempts to control it would be fraught with frightful danger.

ETHERIC PRESSURE
Secondly, there is what can best be described as an etheric pressure, somewhat corresponding to, though immensely greater than, the atmospheric pressure. In ordinary life we are as little conscious of one of these pressures as we are of the other, but nevertheless they both exist, and if science were able to exhaust the ether from a given space, as it can exhaust the air, the one could be proved as readily as the other. The difficulty of doing that lies in the fact that matter in the etheric condition freely interpenetrates matter in all states below it, so that there is as yet no means within the knowledge of our physicists by which any given body of ether can be isolated from the rest. Practical Occultism, however, teaches how this can be done, and thus the tremendous force of etheric pressure can be brought into play.

LATENT ENERGY

Thirdly, there is a vast store of potential energy which has become dormant in matter during the involution of the subtle into the gross, and by changing the condition of the matter some of this may be liberated and utilized, somewhat as latent energy in the form of heat may be liberated by a change in the condition of visible matter.

SYMPATHETIC VIBRATION

Fourthly, many striking results, both great and small, may be produced by an extension of a principle which may be described as that of sympathetic vibration. Illustrations taken from the physical plane seem generally to misrepresent rather than elucidate astral phenomena, because they can never be more than partially applicable; but the recollection of two simple facts of ordinary life may help to make this important branch of our subject clearer, if we are careful not to push the analogy further than it will hold good.

It is well known that if one of the wires of a harp be made to vibrate vigorously, its movement will call forth sympathetic vibrations in the corresponding strings of any number of harps placed round it, if they are tuned to exactly the same pitch. It is also well known that when a large body of soldiers crosses a suspension bridge it is necessary for them to break step, since the perfect regularity of their ordinary march would set up a vibration in the bridge which would be intensified by every step they took until the point of resistance of the iron was passed, when the whole structure would fly to pieces.

With these two analogies in our minds (never forgetting that they are only partial) it may seem more comprehensible that one who knows exactly at what rate to start his vibrations – knows, so to speak, the keynote of the class of matter he wishes to affect – should be able by sounding that keynote to call forth an immense number of sympathetic vibrations. When this is done on the physical plane no additional energy is developed; but on the astral plane there is this difference, that the matter with which we are dealing is far less inert, and so when called into action by these sympathetic

93

vibrations it adds its own living force to the original impulse, which may thus be multiplied manifold; and then by further rhythmic repetition of the original impulse, as in the case of the soldiers marching over the bridge, the vibrations may be so intensified that the result is out of all apparent proportion to the cause. Indeed, it may be said that there is scarcely any limit to the conceivable achievements of this force in the hands of a great Adept who fully comprehends its possibilities; for the very building of the Universe itself was but the result of the vibrations set up by the Spoken Word.

MANTRAS

The class of mantras or spells which produce their result not by controlling some elemental, but merely by the repetition of certain sounds, also depend for their efficacy upon this action of sympathetic vibration.

DISINTEGRATION

The phenomenon of disintegration also may be brought about by the action of extremely rapid vibrations, which overcome the cohesion of the molecules of the object upon which we operate. A still higher rate of vibration of a somewhat different type will separate these molecules into their constituent atoms. A body reduced by these means to the etheric condition can be moved by an astral current from one place to another with great rapidity; and the moment that the force which has been exerted to put it into that condition is withdrawn it will be forced by the etheric pressure to resume its original condition.

Students often at first find it difficult to understand how in such an experiment the shape of the article dealt with can be preserved. It has been remarked that if any metallic object – say, for example, a key – be melted and raised to a vaporous state by heat, when the heat is withdrawn it will return to the solid state, but it will no longer be a key, but merely a lump of metal. The point is well taken, though as a matter of fact the apparent analogy does not hold good. The elemental essence which informs the key would be dissipated by the alteration in its condition – not that the essence itself can be affected by the action of heat, but that when its temporary body is destroyed (as a solid) it pours back into the great

94

reservoir of such essence, much as the higher principles of a man, though entirely unaffected by heat or cold, are yet forced out of a physical body when it is destroyed by fire.

Consequently, when what had been the key cooled down into the solid condition again, the elemental essence (of the "earth" or solid class) which poured back into it would not be the same as that which it contained before, and there would be no reason why the same shape should be retained. But a man who disintegrated a key for the purpose of removing it by astral currents from one place to another would be careful to hold the same elemental essence in exactly the same shape until the transfer was completed, and then when his will-force was removed it would act as a mould into which the solidifying particles would flow, or rather round which they would be re-aggregated. Thus, unless the operator's power of concentration failed, the shape would be accurately preserved.

It is in this way that objects are sometimes brought almost instantaneously from great distances at spiritualistic *séances,* and it is obvious that when disintegrated they could be passed with perfect ease through any solid substance, such, for example, as the wall of a house or the side of a locked box, so that what is commonly called "the passage of matter through matter" is seen, when properly understood, to be as simple as the passage of water through a sieve, or of a gas through a liquid in some chemical experiment.

MATERIALIZATION
Since it is possible by an alteration of vibration to change matter from the solid to the etheric condition, it will be comprehended that it is also possible to reverse the process and to bring etheric matter into the solid state. As the one process explains the phenomenon of disintegration, so does the other that of materialization; and just as in the former case a continued effort of will is necessary to prevent the object from resuming its original state, so in exactly the same way in the latter phenomenon, a continued effort is necessary to prevent the materialized matter from relapsing into the etheric condition.

In the materializations seen at an ordinary *séance*, such matter as may be required is borrowed as far as possible from the medium's etheric double – an operation which is prejudicial to his health, and also undesirable in various other ways. Thus is explained the fact that the materialized form is usually strictly confined to the immediate neighbourhood of the medium, and is subject to an attraction which is constantly drawing it back to the body from which it came, so that if kept away from the medium too long the figure collapses, and the matter which composed it, returning to the etheric condition, rushes back instantly to its source.

In some cases there is no doubt that dense and visible physical matter also is temporarily removed from the body of the medium, however difficult it may be for us to realize the possibility of such a transfer. I have myself seen instances in which this phenomenon undoubtedly took place, and was evidenced by a considerable loss of weight in the medium's physical body.

WHY DARKNESS IS REQUIRED
The reason why the beings directing a *séance* find it easier to operate in darkness or in subdued light will now be manifest, since their power would usually be insufficient to hold together a materialized form or even a "spirit hand" for more than a few seconds amidst the intense vibrations set up by brilliant light.

SPIRIT PHOTOGRAPHS
The *habitués* of *séances* will no doubt have noticed that materializations are of three kinds: First, those which are tangible but not visible; second, those which are visible but not tangible; and third, those which are both visible and tangible. To the first kind, which is much the most common, belong the invisible spirit hands which so frequently stroke the faces of the sitters or carry small objects about the room, and the vocal organs from which the "direct voice" proceeds. In this case, an order of matter is being used which can neither reflect nor obstruct light, but is capable under certain conditions of setting up vibrations in the atmosphere which affect us as sound. A variation of this class is that

96

kind of partial materialization which, though incapable of reflecting any light that we can see, is yet able to affect some of the ultraviolet rays, and can therefore make a more or less definite impression upon the camera, and so provide us with what are known as "spirit photographs".

When there is not sufficient power available to produce a perfect materialization we sometimes see the vaporous-looking form which constitutes our second class, and in such a case the "spirits" usually warn their sitters that the forms which appear must not be touched. In the rarer case of a full materialization there is sufficient power to hold together, at least for a few moments, a form which can be both seen and touched.

When an Adept or pupil finds it necessary for any purpose to materialize his mental or astral vehicle, he does not draw upon either his own etheric double or that of anyone else, since he has been taught how to extract the matter which he requires directly from the surrounding ether.

REDUPLICATION
Another phenomenon closely connected with this part of the subject is that of reduplication, which is produced by forming a perfect mental image of the object to be copied, and then gathering about that mould the necessary astral and physical matter. For this purpose it is necessary that every particle, interior as well as exterior, of the object to be duplicated should be held accurately in view simultaneously, and consequently the phenomenon is one which requires considerable power of concentration to perform. Persons unable to extract the matter required directly from the surrounding ether have sometimes borrowed it from the material of the original article, which in this case would be correspondingly reduced in weight.

PRECIPITATION
We read a good deal in Theosophical literature of the precipitation of letters or pictures. This result, like everything else, may be obtained in several ways. An Adept wishing to communicate with some one might place a sheet of paper before him, form a mental image of the writing which he

wished to appear upon it, and draw from the ether the matter wherewith to objectify that image; or if he preferred to do so it would be equally easy for him to produce the same result upon a sheet of paper lying before his correspondent, whatever might be the distance between them.

A third method which, since it saves time, is much more frequently adopted, is to impress the whole substance of the letter on the mind of some pupil, and leave him to do the mechanical work of precipitation. That pupil would then take his sheet of paper, and, imagining he saw the letter written thereon in his Master's hand, would proceed to objectify the writing as before described. If he found it difficult to perform simultaneously the two operations of drawing his material from the surrounding ether and precipitating the writing on the paper, he might have either ordinary ink or a small quantity of coloured powder on the table beside him, which, being already dense matter, could be drawn upon more readily.

It is obvious that the possession of this power would be a dangerous weapon in the hands of an unscrupulous person, since it is as easy to imitate one man's handwriting as another's, and it would be impossible to detect by any ordinary means a forgery committed in this manner. A pupil definitely connected with any Master has always an infallible test by which he knows whether any message really emanates from that Master or not, but for others the proof of its origin must always lie solely in the contents of the letter and the spirit breathing through it, as the handwriting, however cleverly imitated, is of absolutely no value as evidence.

As to speed, a pupil new to the work of precipitation would probably be able to image only a few words at a time, and would, therefore, progress hardly more rapidly than if he wrote his letter in the ordinary way, but a more experienced individual who could visualize a whole page or perhaps the entire letter at once would do his work with greater facility. It is in this manner that quite long letters are produced in a few seconds at a *séance*.

When a picture has to be precipitated the method is precisely the same, except that here it is absolutely necessary that the entire scene should be visualized at once, and if many colours are required there is the additional complication of manufacturing them, keeping them separate, and reproducing accurately the exact tints of the scene to be represented. Evidently there is scope here for the exercise of the artistic faculty, and it must not be supposed that every inhabitant of the astral plane could by this method produce an equally good picture; a man who had been a great artist in life, and had therefore learnt how to see and for what to look, would certainly be very much more successful than the ordinary person if he attempted precipitation when on the astral plane after death.

SLATE-WRITING

The slate-writing, for the production of which under test conditions some of the greatest mediums have been so famous, is sometimes produced by precipitation, though more frequently the fragment of pencil enclosed between the slates is guided by a spirit hand, of which only just the tiny points sufficient to grasp it are materialized.

LEVITATION

An occurrence which occasionally happens at *séances,* and more frequently among Eastern Yogis, is what is called levitation – that is, the floating of a human body in the air. No doubt when this takes place in the case of a medium, he is often merely upborne by "spirit hands", but there is another and more scientific method of accomplishing this feat which is always used in the East, and occasionally here also. Occult science is acquainted with a means of neutralizing or even entirely reversing the attraction of gravity, and it is obvious that by the judicious use of this power all the phenomena of levitation may be easily produced. It was no doubt by a knowledge of this secret that some of the airships of ancient India and Atlantis were raised from the earth and made light enough to be readily moved and directed; and not improbably the same acquaintance with Nature's finer forces greatly facilitated the labours of those who raised the enormous blocks of stone sometimes used in cyclopean architecture, or in the building of the Pyramids and Stonehenge.

SPIRIT LIGHTS
With the knowledge of the forces of Nature which the resources of the astral plane place at the command of its inhabitants, the production of what are called "spirit lights" is an easy matter, whether they be of the mildly phosphorescent or the dazzling electrical variety, or those curious dancing globules of light into which a certain class of fire elementals so readily transform themselves. Since all light consists of vibrations of the ether, it is obvious that any one who knows how to set up these vibrations can readily produce any kind of light that he wishes.

HANDLING FIRE
It is by the aid of the etheric elemental essence also that the remarkable feat of handling fire unharmed is generally performed, though there are as usual other ways in which it can be done. The thinnest layer of etheric substance can be so manipulated as to be absolutely impervious to heat, and when the hand of a medium or sitter is covered with this he may pick up burning coal or red-hot iron with perfect safety.

In addition to the special forces above-mentioned the principle of the ordinary lever is often used to produce minor phenomena, such as the tilting of tables or rapping upon them, the fulcrum being in this case the body of the medium, and the lever a bar of ectoplasm projected from it.

TRANSMUTATION
We have now referred to most of the occurrences of the *séance*-room, but there are one or two of the rarer phenomena of the outer world which must not he left quite without mention in our list. The transmutation of metals was once supposed to be a mere dream of the mediæval alchemists, and no doubt in many cases the description of the phenomenon was merely a symbol of the purification of the soul; yet there seems to be some evidence that it was really accomplished by them on several occasions, and there are petty magicians in the East who profess to do it under test conditions even now. Modern science is now experimenting along these lines, and will probably succeed in

course of time. It is evident that since the ultimate atom is one and the same in all substances, and it is only the methods of its combination that differ, any one who possessed the power of reducing a piece of metal to the atomic condition and of re-arranging its atoms in some other form would have no difficulty in effecting transmutation to any extent that he wished.

REPERCUSSION
The principle of sympathetic vibration mentioned above also provides the explanation of the strange and little-known phenomenon called repercussion, by means of which any injury done to, or any mark made upon, the materialized body in the course of its wanderings will be reproduced in the physical body. We find traces of this in some of the evidence given at trials for witchcraft in the Middle Ages, in which it is not infrequently stated that some wound given to the witch when in the form of a dog or a wolf was found to have appeared in the corresponding part of her human body. The same strange law has sometimes led to an entirely unjust accusation of fraud against a medium, because, for example, some colouring matter rubbed upon the hand of a materialized "spirit" was afterwards found upon his hand – the explanation being that in that case, as so often happens, the "spirit" was simply the medium's etheric double, forced by the guiding influences to take some form other than his own. In fact these two parts of the physical body are so intimately connected that it is impossible to touch the keynote of one without immediately setting up exactly corresponding vibrations in the other.

CHAPTER V
CONCLUSION

IT is hoped that any reader who has been sufficiently interested to follow this treatise thus far, may by this time have a general idea of the astral plane and its possibilities, such as will enable him to understand and fit into their proper places in its scheme any facts in connection with it which he may pick up in his reading. Though only the roughest sketch has been given of a great subject, enough has perhaps been said to show the extreme importance of astral perception in the study of biology, physics, chemistry, astronomy, medicine, and history, and the great impulse which might be given to all these sciences by its development.

Yet its attainment should never be regarded as an end in itself, since any means adopted with that object in view would inevitably lead to what is called in the East the *laukika* method of development – a system by which certain psychic powers are indeed acquired, but only for the present personality; and since their acquisition is surrounded by no safeguards, the student is extremely likely to misuse them. To this class belong all systems which involve the use of drugs, invocation of elementals, or the practices of Hatha Yoga.

The other method, which is called the *lokottara*, consists of Raja Yoga or spiritual progress, and though it may be somewhat slower than the other, whatever is acquired along this line is gained for the permanent individuality, and never lost again, while the guiding care of a Master ensures perfect safety from misuse of power as long as His orders are scrupulously obeyed. The opening of astral vision must be regarded then only as a stage in the development of something infinitely nobler – merely as a step, a very small step, on that great Upward Path which leads men to the sublime heights of Adeptship, and beyond even that through glorious vistas of wisdom and power such as our finite minds cannot now conceive.

Yet let no one think it an unmixed blessing to have the wider sight of the astral plane, for upon one in whom that vision is opened, the sorrow and misery, the evil and the greed of the world press as an ever-present burden, until he often feels inclined to echo the passionate adjuration of Schiller: "Why hast thou cast me thus into the town of the ever-blind, to proclaim thine oracle with the opened sense? Take back this sad clear-sightedness; take from mine eyes this cruel light! Give me back my blindness – the happy darkness of my senses; take back thy dreadful gift!" This feeling is perhaps not unnatural in the earlier stages of the Path, yet higher sight and deeper knowledge soon bring to the student the perfect certainty that all things are working together for the eventual good of all – that

Hour after hour, like an opening flower,
Shall truth after truth expand;
For the sun may pale, and the stars may fail,
But the LAW of GOOD shall stand.
Its splendour glows and its influence grows
As Nature's slow work appears,
Front the zoophyte small to the LORDS of all,
Through kalpas and crores of years.

For deeply transformative and healing subliminal and self hypnosis CD's and MP3's, plus paperbacks and eBooks
www.subliminalselfhypnosis.com

For powerfully energy shifting and deeply healing and transformative Chakra meditations on CD and MP3, plus spiritual and enlightening paperbacks and eBooks
www.chakrahealingsounds.com

For metaphysical and magickal books, music, herbs, oils, crystals, candles, jewelry, statues and more
www.wejees.com

Made in the USA
Columbia, SC
28 November 2020